M000005332

Praise for
Leading Below the Surface

Read this book at least twice! Maybe I'm slow, but on my second read I was able to go even deeper, providing greater below the surface insights to myself on how I can lead better, and how I can show up with and for others. *Leading Below the Surface* helps you become a more conscious leader, increasing your awareness and desire to create a more intentional impact. It will increase your own understanding of yourself, others and the conditions for a more inclusive culture and help you hone and heighten your intentional impact. Slowing down and digging deeper is central to this book and applying its wisdom, even while curiosity is exciting you to speed up.

> – **Joel Wright**, Founder of the Leadership Forum Community
> and Leadership Development Provocateur in the Tech Industry

LaTonya has been an incredibly valuable resource for us over the last year. She helped me to understand myself as a leader. LaTonya has helped our congregation better understand belonging and the ways our culture contributes to it. She helped us get below the surface in our own organization to strengthen our Diversity, Equity, and Inclusion (DEI) work. I am so excited that LaTonya published *Leading Below the Surface* because I know that many others will now have the same opportunity we've had: for LaTonya to challenge us to grow in ways we never thought possible. Now all of you can access the same approaches that have worked so well for us!

> – **Joshua Fixler**, Associate Rabbi, Congregation Emanu El Houston

In *Leading Below the Surface*, LaTonya combines science with captivating real-world experiences to offer us practical ways to implement the changes that the world desperately needs. Her power comes from a special talent to engage the head and the heart to drive change while staying authentic to ourselves. The *Leading Below the Surface* concept is brilliant and is extremely relevant for all HR leaders right now.

– **Sherry Woodry**, PCC, Leadership Coach and
former *Fortune 500* corporate senior human resource leader

In my 20+ years leading culture-driven corporate DEI efforts, "inclusive leadership" is always cited as a critical path solution. In a remarkably simple mix of deep reflection and research, *Leading Below the Surface* is a practical roadmap for leaders who want to create more belonging in their teams and organizations. By sharing her own corporate experiences with so much honesty, battle wounds and all, we see the literal origin story of LaTonya's research and practice. And it's a familiar story for so many. This book is equally potent as a source of comfort and guidance for anyone who has felt a little lost and empty at work, who wants to belong but can't quite figure out why feeling included is so elusive. In *Leading Below the Surface*, LaTonya Wilkins reminds us that we are humans first, employees second. There's not an ounce of academic pontification or detached theory; the framework is powerful and practical in a way that is only possible when developed by someone who has really been through it.

– **Jane Rosenzweig**, Corporate DEI Executive

As head of Diversity, Equity, and Inclusion (DEI) at a top business school, I know firsthand that DEI initiatives are change initiatives, and leaders who want to make sustainable change in their organizations would do well to read this book. Wilkins' direct and accessible writing provides needed insight into what hasn't worked and what is required to create meaningful relationships across differences.

– **Denise Loyd**, Associate Dean of Equity, Gies College of Business

LaTonya Wilkins opens up a new way of thinking about leadership, welcoming readers to the lessons she's learned over the years—lessons about how leaders can build deeper, non-superficial relationships with the people they lead. She teaches us that leading below the surface not only helps people build better relationships with the individuals they lead and better cultures for their organizations, but the lessons she offers can help leaders build richer and more rewarding careers for themselves. Filled with actionable steps and exercises, Wilkins provides ideas for how to build the skills needed to lead in today's diverse, multicultural work environment—skills which too often lie below the surface, just waiting to be tapped.

– **Idie Kesner**, Dean of the Kelley School of Business,
Frank P. Popoff Chair of Strategic Management,
Professor of Management

Leading Below the Surface

Leading Below the Surface

How to Build Real (and Psychologically Safe) Relationships with People Who Are Different from You

LaTonya Wilkins

Foreword by Amy Edmondson

ACADEMY
PRESS

Copyright © 2021 LaTonya Wilkins. All rights reserved.

No part of this publication shall be reproduced, transmitted, or sold in whole or in part in any form without prior written consent of the author, except as provided by the United States of America copyright law. Any unauthorized usage of the text without express written permission of the publisher is a violation of the author's copyright and is illegal and punishable by law. All trademarks and registered trademarks appearing in this guide are the property of their respective owners.

For permission requests, write to the below address:
LaTonya Wilkins
The Change Coaches, 5145 N Clark, #M27
Chicago, IL, 60640

The opinions expressed by the Author are not necessarily those held by PYP Academy Press.

Ordering Information: Quantity sales and special discounts are available on quantity purchases by corporations, associations, and others. For details, contact the author at latonya@latonyawilkins.com.

Edited by: Malka Wickramatilake and Terri Coles
Cover design by: Nelly Murariu
Typeset by: Medlar Publishing Solutions Pvt Ltd., India

ISBN: 978-1-951591-83-0 (paperback)
ISBN: 978-1-951591-84-7 (hardcover)
ISBN: 978-1-951591-85-4 (ebook)

Library of Congress Control Number: 2021915777

First edition, October 2021

The information contained within this book is strictly for informational purposes. The material may include information, products, or services by third parties. As such, the Author and Publisher do not assume responsibility or liability for any third-party material or opinions. The publisher is not responsible for websites (or their content) that are not owned by the publisher. Readers are advised to do their own due diligence when it comes to making decisions.

The mission of the Publish Your Purpose Academy Press is to discover and publish authors who are striving to make a difference in the world. We give underrepresented voices power and a stage to share their stories, speak their truth, and impact their communities. Do you have a book idea you would like us to consider publishing? Please visit PublishYourPurposePress.com for more information.

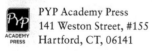 PYP Academy Press
141 Weston Street, #155
Hartford, CT, 06141

Dedication

This book is, first and foremost, dedicated to all my folks who are no longer physically with me. They include, but are not limited to: Grandma Ruthie Williams; my mother, Sandra Wilkins-Carter; my father, Claude Wilkins Sr.; my sister, Michelle Wilkins; and my dear friend, Lisa Russell, with whom I didn't get to spend nearly enough time in this life. This book wouldn't have happened if it weren't for all of you.

Other folks I would like to mention:

My family that helped raise me, especially while my mother was sick, including "the three musketeers," matriarchs who blessed my life until well into their 90s.

All the below the surface leaders who got me where I am today. You know who you are—keep up the real work.

Finally, a special dedication to all the othered folks out there struggling in the workplace. Stay true to who you are. And, to all the good people out there who are critical allies, champions, or simply have good intentions, we can't do this without you.

Table of Contents

PART III

Applying the *Below the Surface* Approach in Your Organization

Foreword

I am honored to write a foreword for this timely and important book. It is timely because our world is on the brink of
historic change. In July 2021, as I write this, we are emerging,
albeit tentatively, from the COVID-19 pandemic. Perhaps the
massive upheaval of the past couple of years has left us with
an opportunity to shake the Etch A Sketch—to erase deeply
grooved patterns to draw a new path together. One path forward from this time of immense disruption, suffering, and
reflection sees us working together to remake our world in
a way that is more inclusive, life-affirming, and sustainable.
Another path is more distressing to contemplate: escalating
conflict and confusion that give rise to animosity, splintering
factions, and promise unfulfilled.

This book is important because our dealings with people
who are different from us in any of a number of ways will
be absolutely central to our ability to pursue the first path.
To begin with, each of us stands to learn a great deal when
we connect better with each other, whether or not we are
"an only," as LaTonya puts it (for instance, the only woman
or the only person of color). It is true for all of us. Whoever
we are, when we are at our best, it is encounters with those

who bring different perspectives to our personal and work lives that allow us to grow, personally and professionally.

But there is even more at stake than our personal growth and development, important as those are. Our problems as a society are now so big and complex that we desperately need everyone's voices, minds, hands, and hearts to solve them. We need inclusion, experimentation, and innovation to forge new solutions. And this means that we can no longer afford to leave people out based on their identity group membership. In a volatile, uncertain, complex, and ambiguous world, anyone (yes, anyone) can have a game-changing idea. Anyone's voice might play a vital role in our success.

But will we hear it?

This is where leadership comes in. Leadership is the force that helps us do what is difficult. And connecting deeply across differences falls into that category.

I am inspired by LaTonya's notion of leading below the surface. This is the kind of leadership that can create the environment where the important work of connecting across differences happens. It points us toward a fundamental mindset shift that comprises the essential challenge of the workplace of the future. Will we continue to treat employees as easily replaced cogs in the machine, as in the industrial-era paradigm sadly embraced in too many modern companies—perhaps most notably by Amazon? Or will we adopt a paradigm driven by empathy and understanding, like the below the surface model LaTonya elucidates in this book? The latter is more difficult, and hence rare, but ultimately far more psychologically and materially rewarding. Those who succeed in doing so will help us forge a path forward that builds inclusion and success.

In my own research, I've tried to understand how people work together effectively across a range of work contexts, including healthcare delivery, tech, pharma, consumer products companies, and government agencies. In each of these different contexts, I've studied people with diverse skills and backgrounds working together to accomplish challenging goals. One consistent finding from this research is that psychological safety plays a central role in their success.

I have defined psychological safety as an environment in which people believe that they can speak up candidly with ideas, questions, concerns, and even mistakes. Consider, for example, an operating room, where a variety of roles—surgeon, anesthesiologist, nurse, technician, and so on—must work together effectively to ensure that a patient receives the best possible surgical procedure. Does everyone on the team, especially those who are not the surgeon, feel completely able to speak up to say that something doesn't look quite right? It's obvious that we hope the answer is yes. Anyone might see something important that others missed.

Although my focus has long been on the importance of speaking up to get challenging interdependent work accomplished, in recent years, I have begun to realize that psychological safety also matters for the goal of inclusion of the diverse perspectives that come from differences. Inclusion is increasingly important in the workplace, as well as in other aspects of our lives.

I believe that psychological safety plays a crucial role in translating diversity into inclusion and belonging. Although diversity can be the result of explicit hiring practices, it's vital to understand that inclusion and belonging do not automatically follow. To begin with, everyone hired may not find themselves included in important decisions. They may not be in the room where key discussions are taking place. Further, it is clear that having a diverse workforce does not guarantee that everyone feels a sense of belonging. For instance, if no one at the top of the organization looks like you, it is harder to feel you belong. The simple fact is that diverse perspectives cannot be heard if they are not expressed, which is where psychological safety comes in. Relatedly, it is difficult to feel a sense of belonging when one feels psychologically unsafe. Inclusion and belonging are table stakes for ensuring mutual learning—and mutual learning is necessary for solving our most challenging problems.

Today, people around the world are gaining deeper understanding of the emotional and interpersonal challenges of building equitable, engaged, inclusive workplaces where people feel they belong regardless of their race, gender, sexual orientation, or cultural heritage. We are also recognizing that these are essential challenges to take on, for any leader today. This is as true for enabling performance as it is for promoting fairness. The tidal wave of harassment claims that started in 2017 showed the costs of failing to create a psychologically safe workplace for women. The past year's accelerated confrontation of racial inequities in society has dramatically increased attention to diversity and inclusion, while also dramatically increasing the ambition of well-led organizations to act swiftly and effectively to make a positive difference.

Great organizations must continue to attract, hire, and retain a diverse workforce because their leaders understand that that is where good ideas come from. But these leaders must also recognize that hiring for diversity is not enough. They must also work hard to ensure that all employees can bring their full selves to work so that they can belong in the fullest sense to the community inside the organization. That is where LaTonya's work is so very important.

To ensure that everyone can participate to the fullest, leaders must get below the surface. The book in your hands offers a road map for that style of leadership. True diversity, inclusion, and belonging will never come from surface changes. Getting out from behind one's own eyes and understanding others requires the force of continued effort. Unfortunately, it is not a well-worn path. Fortunately, we have LaTonya Wilkins and this illuminating volume to show us the way.

Amy C. Edmondson
Novartis Professor of Leadership and Management
Harvard Business School, Harvard University
Cambridge, Massachusetts, USA

PART I

Why *Leading Below the Surface*

Why I Wrote This Book

Those of you who are meeting me for the very first time most likely do not know my story. This book is not about me, but my background and experiences will help you understand why I wrote it and the perspective in which it is written. Many of you know me as the entrepreneur that I am now. However, there was an entire first career that preceded my small-business journey. As a queer woman of color, I have experienced the workplace through many different lenses. In several aspects, I have had a traditional corporate career—I have an MBA, worked in several Fortune 500 companies, and have climbed the proverbial corporate ladder.

At the beginning of my career, I was the very definition of the *surface leader* that I discuss in this book. I would do all the right things and still lose out. I was living on a hamster wheel. When I entered the corporate world as an underdog, I skillfully attempted to navigate my career to reach the upper echelons. One way I hedged my bets was to be closeted. I was careful not to rock the boat. I lived to achieve the highest performance ratings and bonuses possible by working my ass off and "playing the game" while covering up major parts of myself. I gave my heart and soul to these companies.

But there came a time when I couldn't do it anymore. Complying with the unwritten rules didn't guarantee a route to success for someone like me. Between being closeted, seemingly hiding something, and being different from the vast majority of my colleagues, I wasn't invited into the powerful spaces that made careers illustrious. I didn't develop the deep, real relationships that propelled careers. I didn't lead *below the surface.*

After mortgaging my dreams for far too long, the second half of my corporate career was different. I came out. I brought more, but not all, of myself to work. Every year I revealed something new—and with each revelation, I felt freer. The process of growing into myself was not always completely blissful; suddenly, not all of my co-workers accepted me. I felt excluded and even pushed out of some roles because of it. It was a risk, and the very definition of risk is that you win some and lose some.

I had so much to say. Ultimately, I became a professional coach and helped people navigate the very world that was not accepting of people like me. I coached executives to build cultures of belonging, and it wasn't in the traditional ways. We got there by getting *below the surface.*

After several months of executive coaching, I decided I was going to write *Leading Below the Surface*, as I wanted to bring this very approach to more people and do it by sharing my experiences in the workplace. I was first inspired when a publishing company contacted me. They offered to publish my book and provide me with support throughout the process. But I didn't feel like the publisher was getting *below the surface* with me. I felt rushed to make decisions. They didn't truly care about the sources of my reluctance. I wasn't ready and I needed that to be acknowledged. We all experience relationships like this too often, especially in spaces that could benefit most from having *below the surface* relationships.

I have a myriad of personal stories where leaders failed to lead *below the surface* and that's why I experienced a calling to dedicate a book to the topic. I have failed to lead *below the surface* too. We all have. Having spent a good chunk of my professional life in the leadership development space, I have predominantly experienced surface leadership during my career. However, until recently I didn't have a name for it and couldn't put my finger on its effects. In my blog posts (latonyawilkins.com/blog), I often cite studies that measure employees' lack of *below the surface leadership* at work. Consider the following statistics:

- Over half of current supervisors receive no manager or leadership training for their roles.[1]
- BIPOC (Black, Indigenous, and People of Color) folks experience a phenomenon called "emotional tax," which means they exert extra effort to cover up parts of their true selves at work. Some of these exertions are known as "covering," which is downplaying an identity.[2]

---

[1]CareerBuilder, "More Than One-Quarter of Managers Said They Weren't Ready to Lead When They Began Managing Others, Finds New CareerBuilder Survey," PR Newswire, March 28, 2011, http://press.careerbuilder.com/2011-03-28-More-Than-One-Quarter-of-Managers-Said-They-Werent-Ready-to-Lead-When-They-Began-Managing-Others-Finds-New-CareerBuilder-Survey.

[2]Dnika J. Travis and Jennifer Thorpe-Moscon, "Day-to-Day Experiences of Emotional Tax Among Women and Men of Color in the Workplace," *Catalyst*, February 15, 2018, https://www.catalyst.org/research/day-to-day-experiences-of-emotional-tax-among-women-and-men-of-color-in-the-workplace/.

- Only 40% of leaders value and actively practice empathy at work.[3]
- Women, BIPOC, and LGBTQ+ employees experience less psychological safety at work than their counterparts. While employers continue to invest more in diversity, equity, and inclusion, these efforts yield little benefit.[4]

As you can see, this is only a small sampling of statistics. If you Google "unhappy employees at work," you will see it for yourself. It's pretty disheartening. Workplaces and the leaders who run them are deeply flawed. We are all deeply flawed. While organizations spend an estimated $8 billion on diversity, equity, inclusion, and belonging (DEIB) alone, very few have experienced substantive results.[5] I'm not going to spend more time convincing you because, if you are reading this book, you are likely one of these statistics. Maybe you experienced these effects from your own boss or maybe you want to be proactive so this doesn't happen on your team.

[3]Evan Sinar et al., *High Resolution Leadership: A Synthesis of 15,000 Assessments into How Leaders Shape the Business Landscape* (Development Dimensions International, 2016), https://media.ddiworld.com/ research/high-resolution-leadership-2015-2016_tr_ddi.pdf, 29.

[4]Allison Scott, Freada Kapor Klein, and Uriridiakoghene Onovakpuri, *Tech Leavers Study* (Kapor Center for Social Impact, 2017), https://www.kaporcenter.org/wp-content/uploads/2017/08/TechLeavers2017.pdf.

[5]Rik Kirkland and Iris Bohnet, "Focusing on What Works for Workplace Diversity," McKinsey & Company, April 7, 2017, https://www.mckinsey.com/featured-insights/gender-equality/focusing-on-what-works-for-workplace-diversity#.

Leading Below the Surface

What is *leading below the surface* and how can it impact companies? Let's first start with what *leading below the surface* is not.

After I graduated from college, I eagerly joined a non-profit as I was on a mission to save the world. This non-profit ended up being the most dysfunctional place that I ever worked. The executive director was a tyrant and, while I knew my work had a purpose, I eventually decided that my mental health was more important. I spent the next decade in a medley of consulting and people and culture roles. Some of the companies I worked for repeatedly made the "highly admired companies" lists. I searched for *below the surface* leaders in these "highly admired" companies, but only found a few throughout my entire career. Soon, I learned that the more a company bragged about their "high performance," the more *surface* they were. These organizations didn't truly care about their people.

I have always tried to spare complaining and, instead, work through my troubles with a therapist or coach to create the world that I wanted to be in. After my experience at the nonprofit, I wanted to change the world through *below the surface leadership* even though I didn't have those words at the time. I wanted organizations to "see" their people. The system was broken. Organizations didn't truly value their people. Anyone who differed from those in leadership was pushed to the side.

I searched and held out for champions who also wanted to lead *below the surface*. If I found that one leader, perhaps I could change my entire career. I had high hopes. Up to that point, the leaders who I had encountered were what I call *surface leaders*. Surface leaders don't truly connect with their employees and have an especially hard time connecting with people who are different from them. These leaders are hard to trust. They may be narcissists. They are usually about advancing themselves, and when you talk to them, you never quite feel encouraged to bring your whole self to the relationship. Surface leadership is the opposite of *below the surface leadership*.

A few years into my career, I finally experienced a *below the surface leader*—Lisa. I interviewed with Lisa when I applied for a job in a company where she worked. During her company's hiring process, it was clear that Lisa wanted to hire someone who could go beyond merely doing the job. She wanted someone who was real. Lisa wanted someone she could trust. Even that very first interview with her was different; Lisa cared about what I wanted. On one hand, I felt strange being asked certain questions but, on the other hand, I experienced a sense of connection when she asked me things like:

- What motivates you?
- What drains you?
- How do you like to be "managed?"
- What concerns would you have about me as your manager?

I eagerly accepted that job because I wanted to work with Lisa. She became my first *below the surface* direct manager.

Lisa's *below the surface leadership* continued throughout that job and was clearly on display when I learned that, after one year, my position was being eliminated. It was right after 9/11, and the client I was working with no longer had a budget to sustain on-site work. The signs were there even before the attacks. The job had never built up to the expected capacity. I knew it was a matter of time, but suddenly I had no other options as 9/11 obliterated the economy.

I vividly remember the day I learned that my job was being eliminated. Lisa scheduled a meeting. She offered to drive 30 miles to meet me at my office. When she arrived, I immediately sensed that any hierarchy that had existed was gone. I sat at my desk and she sat across from me. In any other boss-employee dynamic, she would have been the one sitting at the desk and I would have been across from her. But not that day. She may have been my boss, but we were going to have that conversation on a level playing field.

Before we even started the conversation, Lisa asked how I was doing. She provided me with words of encouragement, reiterating that we were all struggling, including the client. Then she cut to the chase. She explained that, due to 9/11, the client didn't have the volume of work to keep me busy anymore. She then told me that she had an opportunity for me that might, quite honestly, feel like a step back, but would keep me employed. She could have let me go and let that be the end of it. But she had thought ahead for the possibility of another opportunity for me. Lisa continued to lead *below the surface* even at the moment when our manager-employee relationship was ending for that particular job.

Reflecting on that conversation, I knew that no matter what happened, Lisa always had my best interests in mind. While the alternative assignment wasn't the best fit, I gladly accepted it to continue working with Lisa. That spring, Lisa wrote me a letter of recommendation for business school. That's another thing that *below the surface* leaders do: They give and don't expect anything in return.

Leading below the surface is leadership based on a deep connection. This authentic connection between employer and employee, manager and direct report, leaders and community members, executive teams and employees, can create a culture shift for an entire organization. The concept has broad applications and can be implemented within all organizations, including corporations, communities, and even hospitals. The world needs many more *below the surface* leaders.

A *below the surface leader* is understanding, listens well, prioritizes others over their own gains, has patience, and is nonjudgmental and authentic. They create environments that are psychologically safe. Organizations that operate on a truly *below the surface* level do not need separate DEIB "initiatives;" DEIB is part of the *below the surface* cultural DNA. There is no exact blueprint for what a *below the surface leader* looks, sounds, or speaks like. *Leading below the surface* is different for everyone, and there is no cookie-cutter approach. But at the nucleus of any *below the surface leader* is their keen ability to connect with people, especially those who are different from them. This book focuses on what these abilities entail and why most leaders stay at the surface level. This book is not meant to be memorized, and it's not necessary to try to mimic the "right" way to lead. What I hope you will come away with are some fundamentals that you will eventually apply in ways that work for you.

Very Few Leaders Go (and Stay) *Below the Surface*

Based on life experiences, I have found that the Pareto Principle,[6] which states that 80% of consequences come from

---

[6] Abraham Gosfeld-Nir, Boaz Ronen, and Nir Kozlovsky, "The Pareto Managerial Principle: When Does It Apply?" *International Journal of Production Research* 45, no. 10 (May 2007): 2317–25.

20% of causes, applies to the prevalence of *below the surface* leaders. This is not an exact science; it's observation. In my experience, 80% of leaders have been surface leaders, and I have seen only 20% of leaders regularly go *below the surface*. The proportion of *below the surface* leaders, in general, is probably similar to that of your own life. If you are doubting my numbers, take out a sheet of paper and list all the leaders and bosses you have experienced in your life in one column. In the second column, rate each leader on a scale from 1 to 10 (1 being the leader was terrible, 10 being the leader was great). You are rating the leader from your perspective, but consider the following questions in your assessment:

1. To what extent did the leader make you feel included?
2. How self-aware was the leader?
3. How equitable was the leader?
4. To what extent did the leader encourage you to bring your whole self to work?
5. How psychologically safe did the leader make you feel?
6. To what extent did the leader speak up for you?

Try it. Many people notice that few leaders get high marks for *leading below the surface*. But we need more leaders that would.

Below the surface leaders make you feel like you can bring your whole self to work. They are always finding new ways to connect with their teams. The future of a truly equitable workplace hinges on them.

As stated earlier, I worked for a few organizations that were considered "highly admired" during my tenure. *Below the surface* leaders typically brought me into these companies but there were few counterparts around them. After entering these companies, I quickly learned that my *below the surface* bosses were operating on an island. How could these organizations be "highly admired" if most of their leadership operated at a surface level?

I soon realized that the overwhelming majority of my experience interacting with leaders was just that: surface level. The unwritten rule was that you sacrificed your humanity and identity to say that you worked in these "highly admired" places. These companies prided themselves on being meritocratic, along with having other values such as "speed, excellence, and customer obsession." The meritocracy craze followed me through much of my career. Companies would claim that decisions were fair and that when meritocracy was accepted as the way forward, success would quickly follow. This archaic lie is dangerous to organizations and to the world.

All of these experiences inspired me to write this book. I have seen it all. I've been banished too many times to name. The first time it happened, I was doing great at my job and then, all of a sudden, I was a bad performer. This literally happened overnight, and nobody really explained why. This was after I had played it safe. Turns out that playing it safe was a flawed strategy for people like me.

Another banishing experience occurred when I acquired a workplace bully. She didn't like the way I talked, walked, or approached my work. Oftentimes, she would call me "too smart." I'm serious. She even said that she couldn't "speak my language." These types of experiences left scars, and sometimes I carried open wounds from role to role throughout my career. It took years to overturn the brainwashing trauma that I experienced at the helm of surface leaders.

I'm writing this book because there are far too few *below the surface* leaders, and surface leadership is dangerous for organizations. We need more *below the surface* leaders in the world, and I won't stop until we get them. When you see abysmal employee engagement statistics, lawsuits, and terrible diversity numbers, this all comes back to surface leadership. Surface leadership gets you sued. Surface leadership creates apathetic employees. Surface leadership ruins trust in an organization. Employees don't leave organizations; they leave surface leadership.

How This Book Is Organized

This book is organized into three parts.

Part 1: Why *Leading Below the Surface*—This section highlights why *leading below the surface* will be a highly anticipated approach for many of you and how the structures of human behavior and leadership constructs are holding us back.

Part 2: Becoming a *Below the Surface Leader*—This section provides a detailed path to becoming a *below the surface leader*, the difficulties in doing so, and tips for navigating a surface world.

Part 3: Applying the *Below the Surface* Approach in Your Organization—This section covers the macro level: How can you apply *below the surface* approaches to improve your culture? How can you augment your DEIB (Diversity, Equity, Inclusion, and Belonging) strategy with *below the surface* concepts?

As a professional coach, it's never about our agenda. It's about yours. So, read it how you want. But before diving in, jot down your intentions for reading this book. Are you here to simply learn? Are you on a personal journey? Do you want to change your organization?

Write down your intentions and come back to them throughout the book.

Let's Dig In

Are you ready to rethink everything you picked up in your career about "leadership?" Are you ready to build real connections with people who are different from you? Are you ready to build a real culture of belonging? It's time for a change and, if you are reading this book, then you are ready for it! Let's step into this journey together.

A few notes before we enter Chapter 2:

a. While the stories in this book are real, I have changed names—mainly for confidentiality purposes, but also to focus on what's important. It's not about the company or the person; it's about the approach. Don't worry, I have thanked the *below the surface* leaders in my life (many of whom wrote testimonials for this book), but *below the surface* leaders don't need to be glorified—they do this for a deeper purpose, not for surface reasons.

b. The book moves progressively. We start at a micro (self) level and then move into macro (org) level concepts. The micro section requires the time and openness to get *below the surface* within yourself. Keep a pen and paper handy. I encourage you to simultaneously read this book while applying it. So, if you need to skip around, do it! Each chapter can be read as a stand-alone, but if there are concepts you are not

---

familiar with, you may want to go back and learn about them in previous chapters. If you are in the middle of an organizational change, you may want to skip to the back chapters. If you are focusing on personal growth, you may want to read this traditionally from front to back.

c. I have built in "Let's Reflect" and "Let's Try This" sections so you get the most out of this book. I strongly encourage that, for best results, you resist skipping these sections. Take out a notebook, reflect, and revisit your thoughts throughout this book.

CHAPTER

2

The Flaws with the Dominant Leadership Standard

Several years ago, I was hired by a university-affiliated company to teach undergraduate students, mainly business students, leadership skills. I was looking forward to the opportunity, as it seemed to present a respite from traditional corporate management approaches. Everything the organization did was evidence based, so I was also looking forward to discovering some new leadership provocateurs. One of my first assignments was to compose a suggested list of supplementary readings for my students, and I had to use only books found in the organization's leadership library. I jotted down a few top choices from a diverse group of authors and then headed over to the library to confirm that my selections were in circulation.

The library was smaller than anticipated, about as big as a medium-sized bedroom, so it was easy to dig into. But after only 30 minutes, I discovered a troublesome trend. About 99% of the books in that library were written by white men. In the short time I spent in that room, I came across only a few books written by women, and white women at that. The only books written by Black people dealt with slavery themes. The very few contributions from other cultures were also by male authors. I was suddenly overwhelmed with mixed emotions, but I didn't have time to stay in that state. I snapped into action mode. Copious questions circulated in my head, and they wouldn't stop. I directed my questions to the library director.

Had anyone ever challenged the library? How can they think this is okay?

She dodged any responsibility.

I didn't have time to dwell on it. I often told myself that change would happen eventually.

Fast forward several years, and I realized that that wasn't true. Positive thinking wasn't enough. While I did see small shifts in my own world, that library still looks pretty much the same as it did when I first walked in. The "leadership" industry has experienced little change over the years, and it will stay that way unless we truly acknowledge the ugly truth about where we are today.

But back to that moment of discovering the lack of diverse leadership books and authors. I proceeded rationally. I ended up developing my own student experience that honored leaders who looked and felt like me and my students. I curated blogs and YouTube videos as assignments. I wanted my class to read about different leadership perspectives that the library did not offer and I realized that traditional resources such as books, documentaries, etc. representing me and my students were scarce.

Looking back, I'm not even sure why I was fazed. I was an undergraduate psychology major in college. Nearly all of the psychology "pioneers" were also white males. It's the trend across many fields. While we have recently seen some encouraging shifts, this widely accepted traditional leadership standard mostly remains intact. While it is more pronounced in some spaces including particular industries, countries, and organizations, the tendency still exists. Folks in marginalized groups feel it more than anybody else.

When we refer to "leadership," the expectation, especially in business, tends to be that "the leaders" will be white, male, and, in many regions, Western. But that's not what workplaces actually look like.[7] We experience leadership in many different forms, but organizational expectations widely remain rooted in this dominant leadership standard. This dominant standard leaves little room for diverse voices. In this chapter, I am going to discuss this standard, how it keeps us stuck, and why the presence of this standard inspired me to share *leading below the surface* as a concept with the world.

The Dire Reality of the Widely Accepted Leadership Standard

In 2020, inspired by the #publishingpaidme movement, Richard Jean So, an English professor at McGill University, and Gus Wezerek, a graphics editor for *The New York Times*, took on a unique and much-needed project. They set out to determine the number of current authors in the publishing industry who were BIPOC. It was a makeshift process as this data has not been historically collected. First, they scraped together a list of books that had been written from 1950–2018. Then they searched for books that were held by at least 10 libraries. The third filter was to identify and only include authors published by the most prominent publishing houses.

---

[7]Ashleigh S. Rosette, Geoffrey J. Leonardelli, and Katherine W. Phillips, "The White Standard: Racial Bias in Leader Categorization," *Journal of Applied Psychology* 93, no. 4 (July 2008): 758–77, https://doi.org/10.1037/0021-9010.93.4.758.

Of the 7,124 books included in this study, a whopping 95% were written by white authors. Over the years, the numbers haven't shifted much. In 2018 alone, 89% of books were written by non-Hispanic white authors.[8] Although all of the books included in the sample were fiction, according to VIDA, unsurprisingly, men still dominate nonfiction publications as well.

To understand how prevalent this reality still is, let's do an exercise so you can see for yourself.

My Request of You

1) Run a Google search on the "top leadership books of all time."
   How many are written by white men?
   Women?
   How about BIPOC folks?
   How about LGBTQ+ authors?
2) Search Amazon for one of the following topics:
   "Leadership Books"
   "The Best Leadership Books"

Who is represented within the "leadership" industry?

Through this exercise, many of you may see that homogeneity in the leadership space is a bigger problem than you realized. If you are not white or male, you have already noticed, especially if you work in business, that the vast majority of books recommended to you may have been written by authors who do not look or feel like you. Most "renowned"

---

[8]Richard Jean So and Gus Wezerek, "Just How White Is the Book Industry?" *The New York Times*, December 11, 2020, https://www.nytimes.com/interactive/2020/12/11/opinion/culture/diversity-publishing-industry.html.

authors in the leadership space are white, cisgender, male, and highly educated. When you go one layer deeper, you might notice that many of these authors grew up in upper-class backgrounds. Go even deeper, you may notice that, although you may have gotten something from the book, you and the author have vastly different experiences and perspectives around leadership in general. You may also embody leadership completely differently.

My library experience continued to spawn my curiosity. Shortly afterward, I searched online for the most influential leadership books and found that almost all of them were written by white men. *The New York Times* Best Sellers list is no better. As of mid-November 2020, 20% of the leadership books on this list were written by women; 80% of them were still written by men. At the time, all but one of the authors on that list were white.[9]

When we consider this data, it's clear that there is a prototypical author, especially in the leadership space. There is also a standard, or an unwritten rule, of what those authors should look and feel like. When someone different from this standard decides to write a book on leadership, there is a good chance that the topic or book will be categorized under "other," or viewed as *othered*, and not considered a "real" leadership book.

This is why leadership books that are written about inclusion are often downgraded to a different section. According to the dominant standard, they are not considered leadership; they are "diversity and inclusion," "women's empowerment," or some other made-up category. You might

---

[9]"*The New York Times* Business Books Best Sellers List," *The New York Times*, November 15, 2020, https://www.nytimes.com/books/best-sellers/business-books/.

have to search terms like "Black leader" or "LGBTQ+ leader" because these identities are outside of the dominant standard.

I am convinced that this is why companies have such an issue with diversity and inclusion. We are trying to stuff folks who don't fit the traditional standard into an othered ideology, instead of co-creating a new standard together. This is not sustainable. While we are on this topic, let me set it straight: *Leading Below the Surface* is not a diversity and inclusion book. It's a leadership book. In fact, diversity and inclusion efforts that create meaningful change require a strong focus on leadership mindset and behavior.

The Dominant Leadership Standard's Influence on Organizational Practices

Early(ish) in my career, I decided to get an MBA. My career goals were to learn the ropes in corporate America and to eventually break out on my own. When I finished business school, I landed my first job in a large corporation. It was my first time working in an influential, global organization. One of my immediate observations was that values were the backbone of that company. As I proceeded in my career, I found that this was the case in all large, influential companies. Values drove all the important things in these organizations, including how we were paid, what career tracks we had access to, and even what type of training we participated in. We were even evaluated and rewarded based on the extent to which we practiced and exhibited these values. I will tell you that it was nice to work in organizations that proverbially communicated and held you accountable to their virtues.

But that's exactly what they were: *their* virtues. They weren't ours and, over time, as I moved to other companies, I realized how incongruent many of these were to my own personal values and well-being.

Some of the words used in these core leadership values included:

Speed
Meritocracy
Decisiveness
High Energy
Relentlessness

Trying to align myself with these values was difficult for someone like me. I had never worked in a Fortune 500 company, and I never told anyone there how I truly felt. They would quickly come to the conclusion that I wasn't cut out for it. I didn't want to give any inkling of that, so I kept my critiques to myself. But deep down, I knew I didn't fit the standard.

My Request of You

I want you to be the judge. Go back through the list of core leadership values:

Speed
Meritocracy
Decisiveness
High Energy
Relentlessness

What do you see now? Who do these values represent? Do they reflect your values?

From my perspective, I see a list of Machiavellian traits. A "keep your problems at home" vibe. A hint of "only the best survive here." Whether you sink or swim is up to you. These aspirational values may organically align with some, but they continue to alienate many of us. When this misalignment occurs, those who are othered are left to try and fit into boxes they have no desire to squeeze themselves into.

Some additional themes in the widely accepted leadership standard:

a) **Competition Over Connection:** Meritocracy is a false promise. It states that no matter who you are, if you are among the "best and brightest," you will be rewarded. There are always winners and losers. If you can't get ahead, you aren't good enough. But meritocracy makes us all unnecessarily intense, and it's a lie. Many folks like myself are fooled into believing that if we just work harder, we will be fine. But that's rarely how it turns out.

b) **Baseline Assumptions Are Outdated:** In order to live up to most of these values, your basic needs first have to be continually met. However, in these organizations, that's usually not the case. Safety is a basic need, and if that's not being met, it's very difficult to live up to some of the other things on this list. Many people, especially in othered groups, are simply trying to survive.

c) **Survival of the Fittest:** AKA, it's your fault if you don't make it. Those who are cut out for it will rise to the top; the others will flounder.

Many organizations continue to develop similar leadership values, but they don't apply to a diverse workplace.

They might throw in "diversity and inclusion," "respect," or even "fun" as a value but, many times, those aren't the ones experienced throughout the organization. Competitive values have been widely accepted for decades, especially in US companies. Many companies still conform to the dominant leadership standard when setting organizational values. Let's expand on the standard. Why does it exist in the first place? What keeps us stuck?

Limited Access to Diverse Knowledge, Perspectives, and Experiences (KPEs) Keeps Us All Small

I have had several jobs in corporate succession planning. At one company, Succession, Inc., I was charged with facilitating talent meetings with senior leaders so they could make key promotional decisions. Typically, in order to be promoted to the highest levels, one had to be willing to relocate anywhere in the world. The more restrictions you had on relocating, the harder it was to move around. For example, it was impossible to stay domestically within the United States. If you wanted that, the career moves available to you would be limited.

One particular meeting focused on succession planning for senior leadership jobs and the lack of diversity within the pipeline. At that time, 90% of the talent pool were men. There were only two women in those senior roles, so we zoomed in on their backgrounds. How did they make it? How can we find more of them? Maybe there was a pattern?

When studying the backgrounds of these women, we noticed a common differentiator between them and their male counterparts. Both of the women knew each other and had followed similar paths. This was because one had championed the other. Both women had forged paths markedly different from their male counterparts. Neither of them shuffled their families halfway across the world every two years for a promotion. Both women appeared to stay in their jobs longer without sacrificing success. That got us all questioning: Were the relocation requirements a bit harsh? Are there other ways to do this?

I found it ironic that 90% of the talent pool were men, it had been that way for years, and we were now having a conversation using the only two women as a model. I think that day was the beginning of our long journey of awareness that people of different backgrounds might prefer to have different career paths than the dominant culture. This awareness was only possible because we were finally open and accepting to the idea that people—and in this case, women—might have their own formulas for success. Not everyone needs to conform to the dominant standard. Who people are might influence how they lead and the decisions they make.

Knowledge, perspectives, and experiences—I call these KPEs. The concept is intuitive. People who are different from each other grow up with different knowledge, perspectives, and experiences.

More on KPEs

Knowledge is what we know intellectually. Some people have access to more knowledge and/or different types of knowledge than others. Educational systems are also a factor. There is a variance in what we have access to and eventually learn.

We all gain different **perspectives** based on how we grow up. Perspectives are how we see things. Identities such as religion, race, gender, values, culture, and upbringing all influence our perspectives.

Experiences are encounters that we have in life. For example, people may experience living in multiple geographies, having different types of relationships, or even working in different careers. It doesn't stop there though. A person's experiences can be novel or typical. Some experiences are deeper than others, and some can even be life changing. We may be born into some experiences and choose others. As you see, a ton of variance exists between the types and depth of experiences we encounter in life.

Let's unpack KPEs a bit more using me as an example. I'm going to keep this simple and stick to KPEs that directly affect my career, but know that KPEs go beyond that. Intellectually, I have a Master's degree, complemented by extensive coach training. I have also increased my knowledge in many informal ways, including regularly reading many books to expand my intellectual capacity. Considering that I'm a Black woman who identifies as queer, I've gained many perspectives over the years. One of the most profound perspectives I've had to take is constantly navigating being the only one at work. It's given me a unique perspective throughout life. I also grew up in an environment that was mostly white, so that experience also gave me an unusual perspective that began in my formative years. Now for experiences. Before branching out to work in a business school, my work experience had mainly been in global business within Fortune 500 companies. Through working in these companies, I gained a wealth of experiences. I also have experience as an entreprenuer, which has personally made me more creative and tolerant of risks.

Now let's shift to organizations. If you are in a room of people with diverse backgrounds, they will all have different KPEs. For example, a Black woman who grew up poor and scrappily found a way to make it into the C-suite will have vastly different KPEs than a white male colleague who went to a prestigious Ivy League school, was recruited out of business school, had an extensive tailwind of connections, and quickly climbed to the C-suite. I'm not saying that all white men or Black women are this way, but I purposely use a familiar example to make the point. It's an example that I have personally and repeatedly seen in my coaching work.

Representation and acceptance of diverse KPEs are lacking both in the dominant leadership standard and in organizational leadership as a whole. Yes, there are signs that we are gradually gaining more awareness around this. However, awareness alone doesn't change the fact that, even when organizations bring in someone different, they are still held to a dominant standard that is very difficult to emulate. I often see this during my coaching sessions with folks who are the only ones at work. Companies want to do better so they hire their first Black person at an executive level. But, six months later, that same hire is already drained. They are being held to a standard that isn't authentic to them, a standard that preceded them and was developed by people with opposite KPEs. Unless they voluntarily submit to losing themselves in the process, they are expected to do the impossible.

How KPEs Enhance Our Leadership Styles

As a Black woman, I always wondered when I would come across a Black leader in a proximal position of power, one who directly affected me. I had that chance in an early job outside of school. Finally, my direct manager was Black. My boss also led the entire organization, so I reported to "the big boss." Being Black and female alone didn't necessarily make her a more relatable manager, but there were some differences in how she led as compared with other white leaders up to that point. First off, she led with passion and resilience. She had a very strong "why." Leading the organization was aligned with her purpose, and she reiterated that almost every day. Also, she didn't conform to the dominant leadership standard. She ran late to almost every meeting. The organization moved at a different pace, and she was fine with the mess of it all. Maybe it was a coincidence, maybe not, but her leadership presented a markedly different experience.

My Black manager felt like she was operating just fine and didn't lose any sleep over other people's expectations. Her persona was deeply reflected in her leadership style, to the point that it made many folks feel uncomfortable. Her style was far too unfamiliar, which was a problem for many of my coworkers. Many years later, I realized that she was unapologetically breaking the mold.

While vast literature is not dedicated to this topic, there is enough to suggest that, due to differing KPEs, diverse groups might lead differently. It's fascinating. For example, one study shows that LGBTQ+ leaders self-reported being more inclusive and relationship-oriented.[10] These same leaders were also reported to approach the decision-making process differently, bringing in their "outsider" perspective. In a couple of other studies, Black women reported more distinct leadership

---

[10]Eric A. Bullard, "Queer Leadership: A Phemonological Study of the Experiences of Out and Gay Lesbian Higher Education Presidents," PhD diss., (Colorado State University, 2013).

values—suggesting that Black women leaders tend to embody emotional intelligence, championing staff, authenticity, and resilience more than their counterparts in other groups.[11]

There is also a classic study where Black supervisors were rated higher than their white counterparts on three of the four managerial leadership measures (managerial support, goal emphasis, and work facilitation). In other words, Black supervisors were seen as providing more support to their subordinates, placing greater emphasis on the task to be completed, and removing more obstacles that may hinder the completion of the job. This study is dated, but I'm including it as there's not much research in this area even today as I write this book.[12]

Overall, there is evidence that diverse groups lead differently. This valuable information is not included in the standard. We might be navigating it in pockets, but the effects are not enough to drive systemic change.

There Are Scrappy Solutions, but Not Everyone Has Access or Can Endure Them (and They Shouldn't Have To)

Imagine that you want to learn how to make a casserole. You've never made one before, and you are quickly overwhelmed by the number of recipes to choose from. So you make the task more manageable by studying the recipes that appeal to you the most. You soon notice a trend, that there

---

[11]Laura Morgan Roberts et al., "Beating the Odds," *Harvard Business Review*, March–April 2018, https://hbr.org/2018/03/beating-the-odds.

[12]Kathryn M. Bartol, Charles L. Evans, and Melvin T. Stith, "Black versus White Leaders: A Comparative Review of the Literature," *The Academy of Management Review* 3, no. 2 (April 1978): 293–304.

are "make or break" ingredients. For example, each recipe calls for a base and a sauce. Beyond that, you see that you can really get creative with whatever you want to add. A little spice here, a little sweetness there, a couple of veggies to add some color. Cheese or no cheese, meat or no meat—the choice is entirely yours. Soon, you have your own unique dish that honors your taste buds and satisfies your hunger. You started with a base recipe and made it your own.

Now imagine applying this same process to every single business book you read. Imagine if every book stopped after outlining the base and the sauce. You are on your own from there. *Imagine that with each book, you have to create your own unique recipe. Every single book.* After a while, it's exhausting. This is how I have felt about leadership books my entire life. If you have ever felt like an other, this probably describes you too. But there is an imperfect way to circumvent the exhaustion.

There is a concept in human development that explains how to get around it: self-authorship. Self-authorship is the process of creating your own concepts of experience after pulling from many perspectives. When we are capable of self-authorship, we have a sense of our true personal mission and values. While we seek out many perspectives, we decide what we take or leave based on our own intrinsically formed mission and values. Self-authorship is a progressive level of human development, and it's estimated that only 35% of the adult population is capable of self-authorship. Through self-authorship, we step into our distinct superpowers.[13]

---

[13]Natali Morad, "Part 1: How to Be an Adult—Kegan's Theory of Adult Development," Medium, September 28, 2017, https://medium.com/@NataliMorad/how-to-be-an-adult-kegans-theory-of-adult-development-d63f4311b553.

Othered leaders rely on self-authorship to make sense of their experiences in a world not defined or represented by them. In the scarce literature out there, self-authorship is described as a norm for Black women. It's our reaction to having a lack of KPEs that represent us in leadership science and organizational practices. We have to pave our own roads, as the existing ones constantly lead us to dead ends.

After I understood the concept of self-authorship, I realized that the women at Succession, Inc. had also practiced self-authorship to reach levels never before held by women. They figured out what constituted base level success, started there, and relied on self-authorship to create their own stories. The norm at Succession, Inc. was that global leaders had to move every two years. But these women bent the rules. They would relocate but they would do so less often. They understood the base and added the sauces that aligned with their values.

Self-authorship is a process that has propelled othered folks into the upper echelons of their organizations. However, not all humans can rise to the level of self-authorship. For those who do, it is not an instantaneous process. You may not see results and alignment for years. When I decided to stop conforming, my full self-authorship process took years. Also, the burden lies entirely on the folks outside of the standard. This is why we need a different way to look at leadership. We need to openly access our differences. We need to lead *below the surface.*

Leading Below the Surface as the Most Accessible Solution

Leading below the surface is a novel archetype of leadership. The same way you can be a charismatic leader, a strategic leader, and a leader coach, you can also be a *below the surface leader*. These leaders build real relationships with people different from them so they can nonjudgmentally access them at deeper levels. They do this over and over again. By the very nature of these relationships, they start off on a real footing, and eventually these same relationships evolve, becoming psychologically safe.

If you are reading this book right now, you probably want to lead *below the surface*. What if I told you that most people will never get there? While most people *can* lead *below the surface*, it's difficult to achieve. My fellow coach colleagues often say, "It's not the practices themselves that are tough, the hardest part is putting them in practice." Putting something into practice is where the magic happens.

It's extremely difficult to put *below the surface* concepts into action because we are constantly navigating a world filled with surface leaders. Being surface is normalized, and there are few consequences, if any, to being a surface leader. People want to get better but, as with anti-racism movements in companies, people performatively commit but have a hard time truly changing. While you like the idea and are open to change, it's hard to make real progress. You may get started and experience a "newness" high. But soon, that high wears off and you go back to your old ways.

Leading below the surface is a new path forward. It challenges the very leadership standard in this chapter. Diverse KPEs are regularly sought out. *Leading below the surface* gets you to a level where connection is organic—the type that can lead to a natural progression of equity and inclusion in all facets of an organization. In the coming pages, I will share *below the surface* approaches and examples with you. We will have opportunities to deeply reflect and embody what's next. Let's forge a path forward together.

Humans Were Born to Exclude

I recall the day vividly. I was in the front classroom of my all-white elementary school. We were in art class and I didn't have all the crayons I needed that day to complete my drawing of a young woman with hair and a purse. Growing up in an almost all-white town created all kinds of early childhood identity conflicts for me. At that time, I didn't like the colors black and brown for faces *or* hair. So, in that moment, I eschewed my feelings of discomfort and searched for the familiar: a yellow crayon for blond hair, as that was the color that represented the most familiar beauty. But the yellow crayon was taken. Apparently, many of my classmates had the same idea.

Then a purple crayon appeared at exactly the right time. It seemed like the perfect compromise. Purple was lighter than black but was not quite the same. I immediately started coloring. When I started filling in the lines, the aesthetic looked even better on paper than I anticipated. Purple for the hair. I settled on orange for her face, leaving the brown and black crayons behind. Once I colored in everything, it was time for show and tell. We were all asked to share our drawings.

We went around the room and, when it finally got to me, I couldn't wait to share my character's new hairdo. But it didn't go as planned. As I was showing and telling, Sally, a kid I longed to be friends with, yelled out, "Purple hair! Who has purple hair? And why is the person's face orange? *It's not dark enough.* You are *dark*."

I never forgot what happened that day, even though it's decades later. I felt embarrassed, hurt, confused, and defeated all at the same time. It was my first lesson in colorism. At the time, I had two important realizations. First, I was different from the other kids in my school. I was the only Black kid in my class and I didn't really know why at the time. Second, not only was I different, I stuck out, and not in a way that felt good at all. My differences pushed me straight to the margins. I was denied privileges because of these differences.

From that day on, I continued experiencing what it looked and felt like to be different. I was the last one picked on Four Square teams. I didn't get invited to the important birthday parties. People frequently recalled my flubbed, purple-haired, orange-faced drawing. Meanwhile, my classmates were obsessed with Sally and followed her around everywhere. She was invited to every birthday party, and our entire class longed to get an invitation to go to Sally's house. There wasn't room for purple hair or orange faces. People desperately wanted to be around the person who was popular.

Kids like Sally also had the power to uproot others' playdates. In the middle of a perfectly fun game of tag, my friends would often leave if Sally wanted to play somewhere else on the playground. She seemed to call the shots for everyone. She had the power to get everyone to stop what they were doing and give her their undivided attention.

Reflecting on these situations as an adult, I realized that these kids weren't intentionally being mean. The group was influenced by human bias, and I didn't truly understand what that meant until I entered the workplace. I have worked with several "Sallys," and they were operating on natural human instinct. You see, human bias wires us for sameness and the desire to fit in. We do it at any cost.

I named these two groupings as I went through life: the *core group* and the *othered group.*

The othered group are the folks on the margins. The core group creates the norms, and folks on the margins are left with the scraps. The core group are the folks who are also running the "leadership" industry.

Sally was part of the elite core. She was the most popular kid, so she set the norms, which dictated how we interacted with others. The reason why all the kids followed Sally is because they were rewarded with approval when they followed the norms set for them. There were consequences for those who didn't. We were outcasts.

As I went through my adult life on the margins, I eventually started finding pride in my differences, but it was an arduous journey. I was repeatedly stalked by the same surface behaviors. There was always a core group and the folks on the margins, in every single company. If you were different from the norm, perhaps by race, gender, orientation, or class, you may have been glossed over or even ignored. Soon, you may have felt that you could only bring select parts of yourself to work and, eventually, you may have become so resentful that you left the organization with a terrible impression. Much of this can be explained by the nature of human behavior, behavior that we are all prone to. If we aren't careful, this very nature of human behavior can spiral both kids and adults into a state of malevolence very quickly. The switch flips so quickly that we barely notice what's going on.

Many of the core groups I was shut out of throughout my life were composed of people who were the opposite of me. Most of them were Sallys. Usually, they were mainstream "popular," and many often conformed to unhealthy leadership habits to get ahead. The ticket to entry into these groups was usually something visible on the surface; that's what kept the groups homogeneous. These golden tickets were usually granted based on inherited, visible qualities including skin color, perceived level of wealth, and other surface, appearance-based presumptions.

Let's Reflect

Think of a time when you didn't fit in. What was the situation? What parts of yourself did you attempt to hide?

Jot down your answers to these questions before moving on to the next section.

The Science Behind Not Fitting In

Before entering this section of the book, it's important, regardless of your position, to note your own experiences of not fitting in. We can't be empathetic about someone else's adversity unless we are vulnerable ourselves. Let's be clear. *Everyone* has been misunderstood at some point in their lives and, while one may think that someone else's situation is not as severe as theirs, we really don't know how much any experience may have weighed down someone's life. Everyone has something to share.

When I conduct empathy interviews with senior leaders about times they have felt misunderstood, they tell me nobody has ever asked them that question before. But they don't struggle identifying situations that were difficult for them. Everyone's pain, avoidance, and privilege prevents us from authentically engaging with others, especially people who are different from ourselves. Many folks may unknowingly use their own privilege as a shield. *Everyone has pain and discomfort, and we all have something that compromises our ability to fit in.*

The opposite of not fitting in is belonging and, according to studies, it appears to be a primal instinct. Numerous social psychological theories show that humans naturally need to belong to something bigger and strive to be socially accepted. Belonging is fundamental to our health and well-being. There was even a study done that equated the experience of not belonging to that of physical pain.[14] According to the classic Maslow's hierarchy of needs, you need to achieve a sense of belonging before you can lead a fully actualized life.[15] But sometimes, our longing to belong does more harm than good. Even in homogeneous groups, suffocating hierarchies tend to form, which means that you still almost always have a core group and an othered group. Sometimes, we even exclude to belong, a tactic that isn't nearly as satisfying if one group isn't losing out. Humans long to fit in, so core groups naturally form. That's the science here, and we will go to any lengths to get there.

---

[14]Kirsten Weir, "The Pain of Social Rejection," *Monitor on Psychology* 43, no. 4 (2012): 50, http://www.apa.org/monitor/2012/04/rejection.

[15]Abraham Maslow, "A Theory of Human Motivation," *Psychology Review* 50, no. 4 (1943): 370–96.

Human Biases and Their Harmful Effects on Belonging

We all go well out of our way to belong, often at the expense of others. Leaders dread thinking of themselves this way, so we live with the illusion that we are "open-minded" and have the best intentions.

We may think we are open-minded, but the vast majority of us who say we are actually aren't. Our brains are constantly trying to simplify things, hence our unconscious biases. Shortcuts are efficient. They put us all on autopilot. For the most part, we aren't malevolently leaving others out; our brains and bodies love the feeling of fitting in. When we explore neuroscience, we find that humans release a natural chemical, oxytocin, that makes us feel good and gravitate towards people who make us feel more comfortable, included, and part of the team. Cultivating relationships with people similar to us is just easier, and our bodies like these experiences more.[16] Connecting with those who are not like us takes a little extra work, and our brains may not reward us as quickly or easily as they do when we are interacting with people who are similar to us.

You may want to do the right thing, but what if I told you that the odds are against you? We all innately tend to gravitate towards people who look and feel like us because we want to belong. Our biases start to take control, and we soon run on autopilot. There are dozens of biases in social psychology, but to lead *below the surface*, it's important to

---

[16] Jade Wu, "The Power of Oxytocin," *Psychology Today*, February 11, 2020, https://www.psychologytoday.com/us/blog/the-savvy-psychologist/202002/the-power-oxytocin.

norms be questioned? The company was making money and doing fine.

In this particular so-called "high-performing culture," norms such as "managing up" and "being better than your peers" were at front and center. Culture, Inc. mistakenly assumed that these unquestioned beliefs made their culture great. But subconsciously adhering to norms developed by the core group constantly pushed othered folks straight to the margins. It wasn't possible for anyone but the core group to experience a high sense of belonging. Culture Inc. unwittingly became trapped in a constant churn.

Your Culture Can Quickly Be Based on Superficial Exclusion If You Aren't Careful

Soon after I started my first culture job, I wanted to expand my IQ in this area, so I mined through a barrage of studies I had never seen before. One concept I dug up seemed to capture the good and bad of culture: social control. Social control can be described as a certain set of rules and standards in an organization that regulate our behaviors. Individuals conform to these standards, and conformity is a form of social control.[18] Social control maintains cohesion and regulation in companies and societies.

As you may have guessed, social control can help or hurt your culture. I would argue that the control mechanisms in Culture, Inc. hurt the culture. At Culture, Inc., social control

---

[18] Charles O'Reilly, "Corporations, Culture and Commitment: Motivation and Social Control in Organizations," *California Management Review* 31, no. 4 (July 1, 1989): 9–25.

created a deeper level of exclusion. If you didn't look a certain way or go to a certain school, you were pushed out.

On the flip side, if accessed properly, social control can also fuel positive change in organizations. For example, I once worked for a company where people would shun you if your hiring slates for leadership roles didn't have at least one *viable* woman, intersectional, and/or BIPOC person on it. The candidate slates were public and seen by the entire team and, if you didn't have a diverse slate, you were questioned. It was a norm and a form of social control that advanced the organization.

At Culture, Inc., however, the toxic culture wasn't benefitting the company. These harmful behaviors were deeply entrenched in the organization's DNA and social control reinforced them.

The point here is that when you look at Culture, Inc. from the outside, you may say that it only hires the "best and brightest," and this is why it's not diverse. Looking back at the case study, our findings weren't "typical" of DEIB findings. We didn't look only at metrics; we dug deeper. What we encountered were the usual differentiators that "high-performing" organizations pride themselves on. You can't understand or access these behaviors unless you get *below the surface.* Humans were born to exclude, so if you let things run on autopilot, exclusion is bound to happen. Social control will quickly take over.

Summary: Why All This Matters and How to Move Forward

In order to be capable of *leading below the surface*, we first have to understand the surface behaviors that we are prone to as humans. Next, we have to keep an eye on how biases and social control may negatively affect our organizations. Many companies have developed training that operates under the presumption that if you know and understand bias, you can stop it in its tracks. From this chapter, you can see why this is not the case. *Leading below the surface* goes well beyond that. Instead of an episodic focus on diversity training, for example, your entire perspective will shift. More on this in the next chapter.

PART II

Becoming a *Below the Surface Leader*

The *Leading Below the Surface* Approach

It was a hot summer day, and I was on my way to a meeting of a global professional association I had recently joined. I was stoked. It was one of the first associations I had joined as a business owner, as opposed to an employee. I remember walking in and seeing pockets of tight-knit groups. Cliques. It was clear that people had known each other for a long time. I went up to the registration table to get my badge, and someone boisterously commented, "You must be new!"

I guess I stuck out like a sore thumb. About 95% of the people at the event were white, and at least 10 years older than me. I was skeptical, so I went and sat down towards the back. It was the content that drew me to the event, so I soon decided to just focus on that. Then, something completely unexpected happened.

A white woman with brown hair approached me and said, "Hi, LaTonya. I want you to know that you are welcome here. My name is Louise, and I am the president of the organization. I know it can appear that we are a clique as we're standing in groups because we have all known each other for a long time, but you're welcome here."

I started a brief conversation with Louise about the group and recent events before she was pulled away to tend to other business. Then another long-standing member came over and sat with me. Ed was a tall white man who was decades older than me. He and I soon found ourselves in a deep conversation about everything: our businesses, our partners, real estate investing, you name it. When the event was over, we continued our riveting conversation over lunch.

While I never went back to an event for that particular association, I have to admit that the day was full of unexpecteds. It was probably the first event ever where people went out of their way to make me feel like I belonged. These were *below the surface* gestures, something that I had only experienced on a limited basis. I questioned why I had not had more interactions like that before, because it was not hard to do.

In this chapter, we are going to dive into the *leading below the surface* approach. This approach is heavily inspired by organizational culture research, social psychology, and neuroscience frameworks. Over the years, through studying all of these topics, I coalesced this research with my personal and workplace experiences as a coach. The goal is to change the standard.

As I regularly discuss in my keynotes, I've always been obsessed with why it's so difficult for people to build real and psychologically safe relationships with people who are different from them. Throughout the 50 years she worked in a school cafeteria, my grandmother had real relationships with people different from her in a time when that was very unlikely.

Racism forced my grandmother out of Jackson, MS, in the 1950s, when her daughter (my mother) refused to drink from an infamous Jim Crow "colored" fountain. It was around the time of the Emmett Till lynching. My mother was not someone to tiptoe around societal guiderails. She was destined to challenge "staying in her place" at a young age. My mom often told me the story about how she found herself at a Black Panther meeting as a young adult. She wasn't going to be a "yes ma'am" child. My grandmother saw this spark in my mother and wanted to keep her safe. So, she packed herself and her kids on a bus north—first to Topeka, KS, and then, ultimately, to Des Moines, IA, where she worked in school cafeterias for many decades. My grandma left what had been her home for her formative years, where her grandmother had been enslaved, a place that didn't seem to be getting any better.

We were blessed with my grandma's wise words for her 93 years of life. We grew up with her being very active in all our lives. She told us stories of brutal racism. She also shared personal stories about her co-workers, with whom she had worked for decades, almost all of whom were white. I would hear about their children, their travels, and even their favorite foods. It didn't sink in how close my grandma was to these women until she retired and entered a nursing facility. She loved to take photos and would share those of her favorite co-workers, accompanied by stories about each of them. Some of them continued to regularly call her, even well into her old age. When she passed away, I had the honor of interacting with one of her co-worker's grandchildren. She spoke of how my grandmother had saved her life and had "adopted" her after her mother had passed away.

After all that my grandma had been through, she still developed real relationships with people different from her. The stories I heard from her former students, who were from all different walks of life, were extremely powerful. My grandma stayed *below the surface*, and she inspired me to do the same for the rest of my life.

Leading Below the Surface
Basics—How to Be REAL

I think the reason many people struggle with *leading below the surface* is that we are focusing on the wrong things, operating on autopilot, not challenging ourselves, and not embodying what the research says about building relationships with people who are different from us. We are obsessed with the supposed value we are adding to our organizations, not *how* we treat people. We feel driven by the *whats* (e.g., what amount of money we bring into the company, what new products we launch, what amount of market share we own . . . the list goes on) and treat the *hows* as a luxury. We get to the hows if and when we can. What ends up happening is that the people who truly concern themselves with the hows are doing so on their own accord. They intrinsically want to become better people. These folks want more purpose in their lives; they believe in the power of *below the surface* connections.

People who deeply care are the ones who naturally get *below the surface*—those who don't might need a business case. If they treat people better, what types of returns will they gain? Is it truly worth it? Let the churn begin. This type of "what's in it for me" thinking is not only draining, it is outdated. *Below the surface* approaches (how approaches) are necessary if you want to truly create cultures of belonging—cultures that are defined by connecting with, attracting, and retaining people who are different from ourselves.

Leading below the surface is not only the right thing to do. There are other benefits as well. You will feel more fulfilled. Your connections will be stronger. You will naturally connect better with people who are different from you. Yes, teams will be more highly effective and this will be better for your bottom line—but I'm not going to waste my time writing a business case for diversity. It's time to think beyond this. Let's push forward and do this work for real. Google "business case for diversity" if you need to before believing in *below the surface* concepts.

So, what are the qualities of a *below the surface leader*? Based on experience, research, and living as a person on the margins in corporate America, I have observed four qualities that stand out the most. Remember that this list can be expanded upon and evolve as a *below the surface leader* grows. *Below the surface* leaders are REAL leaders. They are relatable, equitable, aware, and loyal.

> *Relatable:* Relatable leaders aren't afraid to share uncomfortable things about themselves and/or share uncomfortable space with others. They invest a great deal of time seeking out and nonjudgmentally listening to people who are different from them. Due to their significant interpersonal investments, they tend to foster deep relationships, especially with people who are the opposite of them. Relatable leaders build instant trust with others. They are curious, which is why people naturally want to be around them. They encourage everyone around them to bring their entire selves to work.

> *Equitable:* Equitable leaders are committed to and fight for equitable access to themselves, powerful spaces, and other resources. They naturally share power with their staff and others around them, especially those from historically marginalized groups.

> *Aware:* Aware leaders are acutely self-aware and immediately recognize polarizing behaviors that stand between them and others who are different from them. These leaders are also keenly aware of

how unconscious bias, stereotypes, and inequitable structures can hamper their leadership approach. They identify hindrances and take action accordingly. Aware leaders are intuitive, so they also sense and take action when someone doesn't appear to be fitting in.

Loyal: Loyal leaders create environments for success, failure, and innovation. They cultivate psychological safety, allow room for mistakes, and create opportunities for people to redeem themselves from those mistakes. Being loyal does not mean accepting mediocrity. It means that loyal leaders understand that humans are complicated and, sometimes, it's important to forgive and give people more than one chance.

Below the surface leaders are REAL leaders. Relatable, equitable, aware, and loyal are the four most prominent qualities I have seen in *below the surface* leaders. These qualities also align with many other behaviors behind inclusive leadership, psychological safety, and trust. But it takes commitment, hard work, and new habits to get there. For many leaders, the default is to be on the surface, so getting deep can feel like a long and arduous journey.

The Three Levels of Leadership

As discussed, the vast majority of us don't start out as REAL leaders. It takes commitment, new micro-habits, and perseverance. However, when you do choose to finally commit, you will find that *below the surface* approaches elevate your entire team. There are three levels of leadership in the *below the surface* approach:

1) The Surface Level—the shallowest;
2) The Transitional Level; and
3) *Below the surface*—the deepest level.

I often use a sea-level depiction when I'm showing a *below the surface* visual. I became fascinated with ocean-ography after it was suggested that we know more about the moon than the deepest level of the earth's oceans. The deepest levels of the ocean are hard to get to. Some research even says that we are only familiar with 0.05% of the ocean floor. Since oceans are dark and murky, it takes vast resources and a long-term commitment to be able to reach the lowest levels.

Like getting to the depths of the ocean, to get to the deepest and most authentic levels of leadership, we have to commit vast and consistent resources to form real (and psychologically safe) relationships with people who are different from us. Many surface leaders are only familiar with a minuscule fraction of each person they interact with. Surface leaders know basic information about their employees: name, job title, race, and how long they have been at the company. The surface level is the safest, most comfortable, and most familiar area. Many leaders only go deeper when their company forces them to do so.

Surface Level Leaders

"Don't talk about your 'lifestyle.'"
"Don't reveal anything personal."
"I don't understand you. Please speak MY language."
"You are too smart."

This is a sampling of the demoralizing things that surface leaders have said to me in the past. As you can see, surface level experiences are cursory. Many surface leaders operate on auto-pilot and rely on the same flawed judgments and biases discussed in Chapters 2 and 3. Surface leaders typically surround themselves with people who are just like them. Surface leaders are confined to the old-world leadership paradigm. Surface leaders tend to be competitive and solely motivated by wanting to win at the expense of others. They are not interested in knowing anything about you except how you can get the work done. Surface leaders stick to business. They like their teams to run like machines. Surface leaders typically don't deliver real, developmental feedback. The only feedback they care about is the type that makes *them* feel better. They also manage up well, which is why they are often left unchecked. While surface leaders are sometimes relatable, they are not equitable, aware, or loyal.

The paradox about surface leaders is that working for them is not always "bad." Since surface leaders particularly like high performers and workaholics, some similar-minded folks may not dislike working for them. Some people actually like working for surface leaders. Heck, even I did before I knew better.

I've worked for countless surface leaders throughout my entire career but one still sticks out to me—Shayna. I worked for Shayna for a short time but, as soon as we met, I quickly saw that she was very well connected and managed up impeccably well. Shayna was also always providing me with challenging and visible work. She wanted me to look good because it made her look good. Period. When I worked for Shayna, we only discussed things we had in common: work, ambition, and business. I never once brought my full self to work.

My relationship with Shayna quickly went downhill when I unexpectedly lost my sister. As one would expect,

I had a really hard time after her passing. My sister's death was difficult for my entire family, and it eventually tore us apart for some time. It was complicated, and nobody understood. I was early in my career, and things like this were unheard of. Suddenly, I found myself unable to concentrate. I was struggling with everything in my life. At the time, I planned to throw myself into my work harder and push through the entire process. It was what the company taught me. Besides, I only had two weeks of vacation, and that was already spoken for.

Not knowing what to do, I finally mustered up enough energy to talk to Shayna and the conversation was so disconnected that I remember every grueling aspect of it:

> Shayna: LaTonya, what's going on? You aren't the same.
>
> Me: I'm sorry. I'll try harder.
>
> Shayna: Well, I've noticed that you've been off more lately. Some of your colleagues have approached me as well. We've noticed that your performance has been dropping.
>
> Me (*trying to hold back tears*): Everything has been harder than I thought. Losing my sister hasn't been easy.
>
> Shayna: OK. You can take time off. We all have two weeks of vacation.
>
> Me (*Quiet. Thinking that this is not at all reassuring. I say the only words I could muster up*): It will get better.

As time went on, Shayna's issues with my "performance" worsened. She warned me that my lack of focus would insidiously hurt my career. I immediately started looking for a job and quickly networked my way into my next opportunity. Although I was away from Shayna, that experience would leave a career-long imprint that I never would have expected. At that point, I realized that corporate life was a great, big surface world. Overnight, due to an uncontrollable family tragedy, I became too much of a burden for Shayna. The most hurtful part of it was that I realized that my relationship with Shayna was fake. I was there to benefit her; that was my only purpose. In the blink of an eye, our differences divided us and overcoming them became insurmountable. All Shayna knew was that I was a hard worker, and the prospect of anything else—that I was human—was too much for her to handle. She couldn't relate to anything else.

Maybe you have had managers like Shayna throughout your entire career. It's what we expect. We are so deep in old-world leadership that anything else is unexpected. For years, I thought Shayna was one of the best bosses I had, but then I quickly saw that our relationship was fragile and untested. The moment my life got complicated, Shayna was done with me. She threw me in the dumpster. That's the thing with surface leaders—they may seem great until the relationship is tested. Shayna was quick to discard me at a moment's notice when I had a human experience.

One final note about surface leaders. Since they are so prevalent, they are seen as normal and have little reason to change. The only time they change is when their respective workplaces force them to do so (think mandatory processes). But usually, they are delivering vast financial or social value to the organization and are almost always from the core group, so a rationale for change is rare.

Transitional Level Leaders

Transitional leaders are the next proficiency level. They are the norm. I call them transitional because they have a chance to become *below the surface* leaders if they commit to it. Transitional leaders occasionally go *below the surface*; however, they retreat to comfortable spaces when things get murky. Transitional leaders are middle-of-the-road leaders. Their human leadership skills are average, but working for a transitional leader feels markedly different than a surface one. Transitional leaders appear to have the best intentions. They regularly attend leadership seminars and ask their teams to do the same. Transitional leaders can be capricious. They are constantly winning you over yet disappointing you at the same time. While transitional leaders may be relatable at times, they aren't vulnerable enough to be consistently equitable. Although they are more aware than surface leaders, they are afraid of real human muck. Transitional leaders are moderately loyal, but again, when the surroundings get too murky, they retreat to familiar territory.

One leader in particular made me realize that there was even such a thing as a transitional leader: Mindy. At times, I thought Mindy was an above-average manager but when times became hard, she constantly reverted to mobilizing an imaginary shield around herself. Mindy headhunted me to work directly under her. She was impressed with my experience and the potential that I brought to the company. Mindy did all the things that a conventionally good leader does: she talked me up to her bosses, let me take initiative, provided visibility, and even stuck up for me (to a point). Mindy relentlessly expressed her commitment to diversity across the company. When I reflected on working under Mindy, I figured I could do it for a long time. The relationship was fairly comfortable and, basically, whenever I was frustrated with Mindy, I thought it could be worse.

But Mindy had a hard time with being vulnerable. She was also very superficial, and instead of focusing on the quality of my work, she was fixated on things that didn't matter. A couple of times, she made a comment about something I was wearing, insinuating that it was unprofessional. I have to admit that my clothing was on the androgynous side but I was definitely professional. Mindy came from generations of wealth and made sure everyone knew it. This is one area in which we were vastly different. It was polarizing and, eventually, the downfall of our relationship.

At one point, when Mindy tried to change me at my core, I realized that our relationship had plateaued. Instead of empowering me to grow, she became a constant 'splainer. There was too much elaborate advice and I soon became stressed out trying to remember it all. Mindy's philosophy was that I needed to dress, talk, speak, and even do my hair differently—things that would align more with her. Instead of encouraging me to bring my whole self and unique strengths to work, I started to see that she was attempting to make me a clone of herself. There was only one way to present, there was only one way to succeed, there was only one way to write, there was only one way to respond—Mindy's way. If it wasn't her way, then it was wrong. My performance was only as good as the extent to which I put her advice into use. She wanted me to be the Black version of her.

I'm not sure that Mindy could have become a *below the surface leader* as it was fundamentally antithetical to her core. This was likely how she was taught, so it would have taken a full rewiring of her entire brain. She wasn't breaking anything, and she was a traditional textbook leader. Mindy was better than Shayna in many ways. Yeah, she would listen to me occasionally—but unlike Shayna, at least she tried and knew what to improve; she just couldn't get there. She was caught in her lifelong habits.

Below the Surface Level Leaders

Below the surface leaders are REAL leaders. They are naturally relatable in that they seek out relationships with others who are different from them. Their relentless curiosity doesn't allow them to do anything else. Since their networks are diverse at all levels, *below the surface* leaders have an eye for equity. They are always expanding their awareness about themselves by asking for feedback and putting themselves in vulnerable positions. They are loyal and spend time developing others, especially those who experience challenges along the way. They stick with people, especially the underdogs.

As you can see, *below the surface* leaders are wired differently. Some see them as "disruptors." But they aren't necessarily born that way—they commit to it. *Below the surface* leaders see differences in their workplaces and naturally come from a place of curiosity. They are also astute observers; instead of assuming, as transitional leaders do, *below the surface* leaders observe how people different from them experience the world. They pay attention to subtle differences and are always actively working to make their climate more equitable at the individual and organizational levels. *Below the surface* leaders have a knack for creating a sense of belonging amongst team members. They are naturals at creating psychological safety in environments where they lead.

Throughout my career, I have encountered very few *below the surface* leaders. As discussed in Chapter 1, I would say that only about 20% of managers I have interacted with are *below the surface* leaders. I'm speculating that *below the surface* leaders are rare for a couple of reasons:

1) **There isn't a pressing incentive for someone to lead below the surface.** Organizations are still stuck in

incentivizing leaders for activities such as driving revenue, cutting costs, launching products, and hitting key performance indicators (KPIs). I worked in talent management for most of my career and, while we always had leaders set goals, none of these goals were related to *how well* they led their people. Yes, we very rarely did include a few leadership-related questions in employee engagement surveys, but those questions were either more focused on surface level topics and/or leaders weren't held accountable for the results. *Below the surface* leaders get deep because they want to.

2) ***Leading below the surface can be challenging to pull off.*** The concepts aren't complicated, but as many coaches will say, our biggest challenge is our clients implementing what they learn. This will be discussed more deeply in the next chapter.

Although the number of *below the surface* leaders is small, they leave a disproportionately large imprint on our lives. Their impact is also disproportionately large on the world. One leader, Roy, is the quintessential example of a *below the surface leader.*

Roy had hired me, although I didn't directly report to him. Roy represented all of the REAL qualities masterfully. He was *relatable* in that he would ask about my partner on a regular basis. He would also bring her up when he discussed family even though his was markedly more traditional than mine. But I didn't feel any shame or judgment about it.

Roy was one of the most *equitable* leaders I have known. As a prominent white executive, he was a member of the neighborhood country club and acknowledged the access and privilege that fellow members had. Roy was a busy man, and it was difficult to nail him down, even for a brief conversation. Meanwhile, many of my colleagues who were members of the country club readily had the access to corner him and check a few things off their list. Roy would acknowledge this unfair access and would intentionally create access opportunities for those not in that space. Usually, this meant he made himself available via text. He would always respond, and if he couldn't immediately meet, he would commit to a time in the near future. The first thing Roy would ask is how you wanted to spend your time with him. Roy also reviewed his organization each year for fairness and equity, especially in the leadership ranks.

As for *awareness* and *loyalty*, Roy created a culture of open feedback, so he was always aware of his biggest opportunity areas. He routinely collected feedback from all levels of the organization each year and publicly announced his commitments to his teams in an open forum. Roy was one of the most loyal leaders I ever knew. When I experienced a death in the family, he asked me what I needed from the organization and how to make that happen. When I told him I needed a break, there was no judgment. It was completely different from my surface and transitional leader experiences. I was psychologically safe and could do what I needed to do to take care of myself. Roy would also speak up for me, and even when it didn't work, he stayed by my side. We were always a team. We thrived as a team although we couldn't have been more different.

Summary: It's Not Easy to Be a *Below the Surface Leader* 100% of the Time

In this chapter, you learned that the three levels of leadership are: *Surface, Transitional,* and *Below the Surface.*

You also learned examples of what each level looks like. One note I will make on the leadership levels: I have found that there is fluidity between the levels. For example, a transitional leader may occasionally get *below the surface*. Surface leaders may sometimes progress into inconsistent transitional leaders. The point is that it's uncommon to be a *below the surface leader* 100% of the time. Just because you are one type of leader in some situations doesn't mean you are that way in all of them. This is why it's important to understand the *below the surface* approach, REAL leadership, and how to reflect on your progress early and often.

Another threat often presents setbacks: We live in a surface world, so the odds are stacked against us. More on surface leaders and how to navigate a surface world in Chapter 5.

Navigating a Surface World

I was smack in the middle of a job search that was forced upon me. Suddenly, the organization I was working for underwent a bunch of changes, rehauling its entire leadership team. I had already put my heart and soul into making the predecessors happy and didn't have the energy to do it all over again. The new regime was making unreal demands on me, and I was done. I was ready to let this experience go, turn the page, and move closer to bringing my entire self to work. I was inspired by the prospect of finally finding a copacetic workplace for me. But a couple of months into this galvanizing journey, I swiftly had some stark wake-up calls.

We live in a surface world, one in which I would always be on the defense, protecting myself. This was one of my biggest lessons in life. I had to go through it expecting that being surface was the norm, and after one particular day, that's exactly what I did.

It was a hot summer day, and I was getting suited up to head into my final interview. A few months before that, I was referred to interview for a director-level role at a professional services company. Immediately after I met the recruiter, she fast-tracked me to the business leaders, then to the chief people officer (who would be the boss of my prospective boss). All the feedback was encouraging, and the last step was for me to meet in person with my would-be boss. It seemed at that point that the role was mine to lose. The recruiter gushed about me and discussed how well I was going to fit with the team. This last step was all but a formality.

I remember walking into the lobby for that interview. I entered the local headquarters, which was in a renovated downtown Chicago high-rise, and my soon-to-be-boss was stationed on the 30th floor. He was the only one in the office that day from his team, so he took an elevator down to meet me.

I heard the elevator chime and soon the man who I had scoped out online was standing in front of me. Based on my other interviews, I expected a warm welcome, but that's not what I got at all. My "soon-to-be" manager looked me in the eye only once that day and it was to study me, my persona, my outfit, everything about me. I felt him immediately look me up and down in disgust.

Did he think I looked too gay? Did he believe I wore the wrong color? Did he not expect this type of Black woman?

That probably was the most tortuous "interview" I ever had in my life. Not only was it extremely awkward, but about five minutes in, he was attempting to talk me into taking another job I hadn't applied for. The worst part about it was that the plan B job didn't even exist. He wanted to hold me on standby until he could get the headcount to open it. The job wasn't even of interest to me—it was a step back. I was in agony and waited for it all to be over. Thirty minutes with him may as well have been 30 years of my life gone. I studied the hands on the clock, but they never moved fast enough that day.

This was the second time in two months that I had been sized up with disdain, both times by white men who apparently were either disgusted by or wildly uncomfortable with me. Both of them checked out of the interview early on. When I talked to my fellow othered folks, I learned that they too had similar experiences. We had shown up to job interviews, didn't "look the part" (even though we followed everything by the book), and were quickly pushed to the margins in real time. This happened before any words were even exchanged.

There is a stat that I constantly heard in corporate training surrounding first impressions. Basically, according to research, first impressions take anywhere from a tenth of a second to 30 seconds. Not long. Research says that someone has made up their mind about you in less than half a minute. How much more surface can you get?

We live in a surface world. I'm writing this book at what I hope is on the heels of a pandemic, and even though this is considered a "historic time" for DEIB initiatives, people, especially those historically on the margins, are still struggling more than ever. As an executive coach with intersectional identities, I probably see it more than others. Over and over again, I've learned that the hardest part of being a *below the surface leader* is navigating a surface world. How do you navigate a world full of people who banish you without giving you a chance? Even if you are a *below the surface leader*, chances are that most of the people around you: a) don't know what that means; b) don't understand the impact surface behaviors are having on their workplace; and/or c) are so caught up in surface mindsets that it will be very difficult to change.

In this chapter, we will discuss what a surface world looks like, how to navigate a surface world, and how to stick to your *below the surface* mindset within a naturally incongruent world. It's a difficult feat but the good news is that you don't have to do it alone.

What Is a Surface World?

A surface world is one full of surface leaders, leaders who aren't REAL leaders.

Here's the reality:

- Most organizations were built and scaled by surface leaders.
- Those same leaders willingly associate only with others just like them.
- Leaders are biased towards surface behaviors when they are constantly surrounded by others like them.
- Surface behaviors are not limited to the workplace; they also permeate community groups, classrooms, sports teams, and pretty much any environment where a group of people need to work together.

Why is this reality so hard to change? As discussed in Chapter 4, for the most part, leaders are not incentivized to become *below the surface* leaders. Companies are obsessed with initiatives: DEIB initiatives, "great culture" initiatives, "fun" initiatives. It's rarely high on an organization's list to focus on developing *below the surface* leaders, which is ironic because this strategy would actually lead to all the things organizations want:

A more diverse workplace.
A culture of belonging.
Diverse leadership.

It's a novel experience to encounter the opposite of a surface world—a *below the surface* world.

Let's Reflect

To help you visualize how you may have experienced a surface world in your own life, I want you to think back to the last person who told you they loved their job—that person who felt like they could bring their whole selves to work (if desired) and that their differences were accepted. They recounted stories about countless extraordinary leaders who made a game-changing difference in their lives. They regularly felt fully seen.

When you actually sit and think about it, there are probably very few names that come up. This is because the *below the surface* experience is a novel one.

The fact is, the vast majority of our leaders are just . . . meh. Their annual bonuses take precedence over how they treat people. The research supports this. According to Gallup, only about one-third of employees are actively engaged at work.[19] That means that a solid majority of employees are not engaged. Here is a snapshot of the extent to which employees agreed with the following statements most aligned to *below the surface* behaviors, and it isn't pretty.

Each question is followed by the proportion of employees who agree:

---

[19]*State of the American Workplace 2017* (Gallup, 2017), https://www.gallup.com/workplace/238085/state-american-workplace-report-2017.aspx.

- My supervisor, or someone at work, seems to care about me as a person: 4 in 10.
- At work, my opinions seem to count: 3 in 10.
- In the last six months, someone at work has talked to me about my progress: 3 in 10.[20]

And it's not just Gallup. Numerous surveys show that although lucrative investments are continuously being made, these engagement numbers shift very little year over year. It doesn't matter if you pull 2010 or 2021 surveys. The results in most organizations have changed little over a decade. If someone is at a *below the surface* level, it's so viscerally rare that we always tell others. Think about it. How happy are you when you find a place where you fit almost perfectly? Or, has that even happened for you? Have you ever instantly felt like you belonged? It's rare, especially when you are part of an othered group. It's a celebration in and of itself when you feel like you belong and don't have to work at it or pretend. You are immediately accepted.

This is what living in a *below the surface* world looks like. If this feels like a dream, you are stuck in a surface world.

Tell-Tale Signs that You Are Trapped in a Surface Situation

We live in a surface world. But how do you know when you are trapped in a surface situation? There are four symptoms of being "surfaced." Keep in mind that it's hard for leaders to change later in life, especially surface leaders. Once you realize you've been trapped, know that by applying *below the*

---

[20]Gallup, *State of the American Workplace 2017.*

surface tactics, you will be adequately equipped to navigate a surface world.

Four ways to spot surface situations:

1) **Your intuition tells you that you have to hide parts of yourself.** You feel like something isn't right and that you will be punished and/or excluded for your differences.
2) **The leader in question can't seem to connect on a human level.** Every communication seems very calculated and mechanical.
3) **The leader in question is having a difficult time interacting with you.** The person isn't making eye contact, actively listening to you, or acting fully engaged with you. They don't seem to struggle as much with people similar to them as they do with you.
4) **Your relationship with the leader feels shaky, delicate, and as if they can walk off at any time.** Like my experience with the interview that I shared earlier in this chapter, the person has the audacity to be ready to check out at any time. There's no commitment whatsoever.

You may read these and realize that you experience some or all of these behaviors regularly, perhaps even every day. This means you are trapped in a surface situation. Recognizing your entrapment is the first step to navigating a surface world. It's important to not ignore it and I will offer up some reassurance—you do have options.

How to Navigate a Surface World: A Case Study

How do we navigate surface situations without getting worn out and eventually throwing in the towel? First off, we have to cling to our *below the surface* behaviors even in the most challenging of times. Let's expand on what preceded those job interviews.

I had spent many years of my career working in corporate talent management roles as well as preparing leaders for and facilitating talent review meetings. As you can imagine, these meetings were full of many of the biases I mentioned in Chapter 3. Nothing interesting was accomplished because surface behaviors ran wild. People discussed their talent and others followed along. The same good ol' boys were discussed and tagged for future roles. Mavericks, big shots, rising stars, and other masculine commendations were in ample usage while othered folks were pushed to the margins. People who weren't like them or didn't hang out in their spaces received lower ratings, on average. The commendations were replaced with what I call "wells . . ."

> "Well . . . I'm not sure if she can work the hours that we need her to put in."
>
> "Well . . . I'm not sure if he really wants to be here."
>
> "Well . . . I can't put my finger on it, but something about her just doesn't fit."

But the "wells . . ." seemed to miraculously disappear when discussing people similar to the leaders. And, if "wells . . ." did arise, suddenly leaders were more solution oriented. They *could* put their finger on exactly what was needed. Sample responses included for those aligned with the core group:

"He's a hard charger and puts in the extra work. You probably don't know him well enough."

"Our kids go to the same school. He's a great father and individual."

"He's not a great fit right now, but I can personally help him get to where we need him to be."

These same grandiose offers weren't put forth for othered folks. I wasn't surprised. These meetings cemented just how wildly surface the world was. I wasn't really permitted to say much. I could challenge them but probably only had a couple Get Out of Jail Free cards. Beyond that, I was forced to sit and nod my head. It was the nature of my role as a facilitator.

Many people ask me how I did it. How did I navigate a surface world and eventually find my way into a workplace where I could bring as much of myself to work as I desired? I did it by sticking to a *below the surface* mindset.

First, I learned to trust my intuition. For a while I was afraid of it, but I learned to tap into and trust it over the years. It was scary to come to terms with needing to leave or to not take a job. In those situations, I knew deeply that I alone wouldn't be enough to create real change. Second, I had to set *below the surface* boundaries. I had to protect my own sanity. Third, I had to believe that things would get better if I stayed *below the surface*. I would experience more meaning and would do my best and realest work *below the surface*. All along the way, I had to surround myself with as many *below the surface* leaders as possible, which takes a level of *below the surface* consistency in itself. More on all of these in the next section.

How to Stick to Your *Below the Surface* Mindset in a Naturally Incongruent World

I would imagine that the bulk of us have been stuck in surface environments. Maybe you believe that you don't have the power to change this situation. Or, maybe the reality is that you aren't invited into spaces where you can practice *below the surface* behaviors. Anyone can stick to a *below the surface* mindset, even in the worst of situations. You might not have power or a fancy title, but you can still do it. I assure you that you can navigate this world with dignity.

Trusting Your Intuition

With the emergence of data analytics in business, people seem less willing to trust others' intuition as readily as they would a PowerPoint full of numbers, simulations, charts, graphs, and even algorithms. However, research confirms that relying on our intuition is key to building, discerning, and deepening relationships. Personal growth-based fields, such as coaching and therapy, even cite intuition as a foundational practice.

Intuition is also foundational to getting and staying *below the surface*. It is your greatest tool to achieve realness. Intuition has often been referred to as an undervalued sixth sense. It may not be easy to tap into and follow your intuition, but when you don't, you are destined to be confined to surface environments. Take the story of one of my clients, for example.

Tamika was a rising professional who was starting to gain recognition in her industry. While she wasn't looking to make an active change, a large company that wasn't on her radar called her up and asked if she was interested in interviewing for a role and an opportunity for a promotion. Tamika felt flattered that she even got such a call and decided to go through the process. She was most intrigued by the money the position offered. But after the first few interviews, Tamika had an unsettling feeling. The interviews felt rushed and like there was something missing. The experience felt very surface. The first inklings of her intuition were kicking in.

Two weeks later, Tamika received an offer for a 50% increase in pay. She still felt that something was off, but Tamika accepted the job and agreed to move across the country. When Tamika showed up to work on day one, it seemed like nobody remembered that she had been hired. She didn't have the technological resources she needed (they had been shipped late). So, halfway through her first day she texted her boss, who called her immediately. Her boss quickly apologized about her subpar experience and she and Tamika agreed to a renewed onboarding plan going forward.

Still, all throughout the first month, Tamika knew that she had made a mistake. She was surrounded by surface leaders, and it appeared there was no turning back. She was not being seen at all. But Tamika didn't give up. She was hoping that things would change after the conciliatory phone call with her boss.

Two months later, Tamika was laid off. Her boss stated that the company was downsizing across the board, and since she was one of the most recent hires, they had to let her go. Tamika was devastated. She wished she had listened to her gut in the first place.

Let's Reflect

How do you identify with Tamika? Has something similar happened to you? What's coming up for you?

We all have been where Tamika has been. An opportunity falls into our lap, we don't listen to our instincts that the job isn't for us, and we let surface promises, like more pay or status, take over. I understand that sometimes we have to take a job to pay our dues, or we may need the money to support our families. If you are in these situations, it's important that you first acknowledge that the environment might be surface so you can navigate it accordingly. If you go into a state of denial and suppress your intuition, you will end up on the surface just like everyone else. Know and accept the reality. Tap into and follow your intuition.

In this situation, Tamika didn't follow her *below the surface leader* intuition. She knew this wasn't going to end up in a good place, yet she still accepted the job. Intuition is an important practice to embrace when navigating a surface world.

Setting *Below the Surface* Boundaries

The next strategy to apply when navigating a surface world is setting *below the surface* boundaries. Many of us can't simply walk away from surface situations. We may need that job or promotion simply to survive. So, in the meantime, the way to protect ourselves is to set some *below the surface* boundaries. Setting boundaries not only protects our energy, it also sends a clear signal to surface leaders. I have seen people manage to stay at surface jobs for years, without compromising their *below the surface* mindset, as they set clear boundaries and stick with *below the surface* leaders.

Consider the story of Sheila. Sheila was one of the only Black women at her job. For the first couple of years, Sheila worked for a *below the surface* boss, Seth. Seth's three strongest qualities were reliability, equity, and loyalty. He always had faith in Sheila and helped her succeed within the firm. He gave her access to visible assignments and responsibilities. He related to her on deep levels. Sheila even felt comfortable opening up to him about a difficult pregnancy. Seth helped shift her priorities so she could get through it. But two years into her job, Sheila was reorganized to a new manager, Matthew.

Matthew had never managed people before. He ended up being very surface. Matthew had been promoted out of a leadership program cohort, so he had many close relationships with other men in that program. Sheila described it as a "bro culture." Matthew ended up creating roles for many close male colleagues on his team, leaving Sheila behind. Soon, Sheila hired me as a coach to evaluate whether or not she should stay. Through six months of coaching, Sheila built up some boundaries while surrounding herself with other *below the surface* leaders in the firm. She stayed connected to Seth and got closer to the chief managing officer, Janie, one of the only women in the C-suite. Sheila decided to put up some *below the surface* boundaries that looked like this:

- She met with Matthew only when needed. They set up a weekly 1:1 and she kept it focused on what she needed from him to get her job done.

- Sheila stopped expecting that Matthew would change. After providing Matthew with an opportunity to discuss a personal challenge and being disappointed at the result, Sheila set a boundary and would instead go to Seth or Janie.
- Sheila decided to stay at her job. Things like staying close to *below the surface* leaders kept her going.

Employees working in organizations that lack *below the surface* leaders can stay at companies for years when they set boundaries. If you are feeling trapped, start setting them today. Start expecting consistency instead of a fundamental behavior change.

Remind Yourself that *Below the Surface* Behaviors Make for a Happier, Healthier Life

It's very difficult not to conform to surface behaviors when everyone around you is doing it. We live in a surface world. Sometimes, it may feel like it's better to throw in the towel rather than spar with surface leaders. I have been there, too, but will tell you that *below the surface* is the way to go if you want to experience a happier, healthier life. The research confirms it. My client work confirms it. My own journey confirms it. Getting *below the surface* doesn't happen fast, but it surely does last. Do you want to buy the house that went up quickly or the one that went up slowly and deliberately? The truth is that the latter will be more durable and fulfilling.

More on Surrounding Yourself with
Below the Surface Leaders

The intricacies of surrounding yourself with *below the surface* leaders are important. I believe that the future of business is community. Communities transform careers. We have many different types of communities: identity communities, home communities, learning communities, and accountability communities, to name a few. However, to get invited into REAL communities, we have to be REAL ourselves.

Something that I have experienced (and my clients have as well) is that my community was transformed when I got honest with myself. When I decided to be REAL. When I decided to stay *below the surface* in everything I did, I created a *below the surface* community. This community shielded me against the temptations of taking surface shortcuts, like cutting corners to achieve faster surface results. I stopped second-guessing myself when a surface leader appeared to be more successful than me. I looked inward into my community and soon was reminded that being surface always looks good on the outside, but things are often hollow once you go deeper.

The day-to-day won't be easy at first, but I will reassure you that deciding to stay *below the surface* will be one of the best decisions you will make. In that space, you will access and attract other *below the surface* leaders. This community will take some time to build, but it will surely keep you on track. You might only start off with one person, but your community will experience steady growth. Again, let's go back to the house: Do you want the quickly built, low-quality house, or the one that took a little longer and is more durable? If you choose the former, you will eventually end up with a community full of empty suits.

Summary: What Does This All Have to Do with *Leading Below the Surface*?

It is imperative to understand the nuances of a surface world if we are going to break the mold and lead *below the surface*. A surface world is always full of ammunition, and it is necessary to have the tools to navigate through that. Once we learn that we live in a surface world and understand how to make our way through it, we can start our journey into *below the surface leadership*. This takes us to our next chapter, Becoming a *Below the Surface Leader*. We are moving from enduring to becoming.

CHAPTER 6

Becoming a *Below the Surface Leader*

There is a start-up saying that goes something like this: "It's not about the idea, it's about the execution." This saying fits well with *below the surface leadership*. The concepts behind becoming a *below the surface leader* aren't rocket science, but the execution is tough. If you are someone who is a professional-development nerd, I'm sure this is not your first time hearing these sorts of concepts. But becoming a *below the surface leader* is another story.

Below the surface leaders are not the norm, so it can always feel like we are pushing against a brick wall. It's a journey and a constant process of push and pull. While it can be ponderous, committing to developing new habits always gets us there. We are on a fruitful journey that will prove to be both personally and professionally fulfilling. With a little time investment each day, your approach will become intuitive.

What happens when you become a *below the surface leader*? The notable changes you see may include the following:

- The way you approach leadership will be less formulaic. You won't have to memorize concepts; building REAL relationships will naturally come to you.
- You will have more clarity about your purpose and will be immersed in it every day. This will make you uniquely positioned to serve the world in ways that are both useful and personally fulfilling.
- You will build extraordinarily diverse communities. These relationships will be real and empowering.
- *Below the surface leadership* will be a part of all of your interactions (inside and outside of the workplace).
- Since *below the surface* concepts overlap with DEIB approaches, separate initiatives won't be necessary. DEIB will be natural and integrated with your leadership philosophy.

But how do you know how far you are from becoming a *below the surface leader*? In this chapter, we will discuss specific tactics to become a *below the surface leader*. We will focus on the essentials of becoming a *below the surface leader* from an individual perspective. While moving through this chapter, you may find it useful to take out a pen and sheet of paper as a space to reflect.

The Steps to Becoming a *Below the Surface Leader*

In Chapter 4, we discussed the definition of surface. Surface leaders are cursory. They are "stick to business" leaders who rarely bring empathy into the workplace. Becoming a *below the surface leader* instead is a continuous process. Although there are three steps to get there, they may not cleanly happen in sequence.

How do you know how surface you are?

The ultimate measuring stick is the REAL approach. We learn through assessing how REAL we are or our *realness level*. Once we understand our realness level, it's important that we engage in reflection, community learning, more practice, and repeating the process.

Here are the steps to becoming a *below the surface leader* in more detail:

1) **Understand and Assess Your Realness Level:** The goal is not to get to a precise number or score; it is to gain awareness and insight on your progress.

2) **Move from Learning to Becoming:** Now that we have discussed what a *below the surface leader* is, it's time to put the concepts into practice.

3) **Share Your Slips:** Share vulnerably while remaining loyal to the process.

The next section will focus on how to apply each step.

Assessing Your Realness Level

As discussed in Chapter 4, REAL leaders are relatable, equitable, aware, and loyal. Your realness level is the sum of the extent to which you practice each of these *below the surface* behaviors. Let's dig deeper into each behavior in the REAL approach.

Relatable: People flock to relatable leaders. These leaders are particularly good at three things: active listening, curiosity, and a practice that I call *bridging*. Bridging is the practice of taking progressive actions to make and deepen *below the surface* connections over time.

I want you to imagine that you are on foot and getting ready to cross a bridge over a small river. It's old and rickety but still works. There is no other way to cross the river than by using the bridge. Now, I want you to imagine crossing the bridge slowly, step by step. Imagine that you are walking towards someone with whom you want to connect better and that they have to give you permission to take each subsequent step. With each *below the surface* action, you can move closer. The more powerful the action, the more steps you can take at one time.

This is the process of bridging; a process in which each *below the surface* action creates more trust, leading to permission to get closer. Soon, you will be welcomed to cross the bridge and, eventually, be invited to bring others across.

Now, let's explore a relatable leader example in more detail.

Allie is an example of a leader who was exceptional at bridging and was relatable overall. Allie's true superpower was mediating conflict. She was also known for being a champion of a diverse group of folks. Allie was really good at working with her colleagues to build bridges, and then helping them walk across them. Her secret to forming real connections with others who were different was her ability to bridge well. When people would reveal something personal to Allie, she would say something that would bring them closer. She had a knack for bridging behavior.

I remember my own experience with Allie. At the time, I was very closeted at work. One day, I needed to leave the office early to celebrate my partner's birthday. I was too excited to keep it to myself that day, so I found myself blurting out why I needed to leave a bit early.

"I'm taking my partner to a concert tonight and it's a surprise. *She* has no idea!" I didn't know what to expect next but Allie, to my surprise, said,

> "Those are the best birthdays. I'm sure *she* will be excited. Why don't you leave even earlier? None of this work is urgent."

Allie's reaction allowed *me* to give *her* permission to take several steps forward on the bridge. I had a few other stressful situations in my life at the time, and Allie continued to take steps forward on that very bridge. I had recently stopped drinking alcohol and was very nervous about a big company event coming up that revolved around debauchery. Instead of staying in my head about that extreme nervousness, I decided to have a conversation with Allie about how to handle things.

I braced myself. Instead of judging me, she said, "Yeah, sometimes we find that things don't suit us anymore. I think that you are bringing up some good points. What if people don't want to drink? For any reason? Maybe we need more options at these events."

Allie fully crossed the bridge that day. I wasn't the only person who Allie effectively bridged. She became known for it. Allie was also an outstanding, laser-focused listener who chose curiosity over judgment.

Based on Allie's example, how far are you away from being relatable?

Let's Reflect

Use the following scale to evaluate yourself (scale from 1 to 5):

1 = Doesn't sound like me at all.
5 = Very much sounds like me.

1) Listening skills
   - I "play back what I hear" to check for understanding in conversations.
   - I value having conversations without distractions.
   - I listen to learn and not to judge.
2) Curiosity
   - I regularly ask open-ended questions.
   - I seek permission before I give advice or make suggestions.
   - I am curious about differences and am careful not to label them as positive or negative.
3) Inviting in *below the surface* relationships
   - I invite others to bring their entire selves to our relationship.
   - I respond expansively to people when they reveal vulnerable identities and/or experiences.
   - I find unconventional ways to connect with people who are different from me.
   - I inquire about people's interests or life outside of our professional relationship (family, interests, challenges, etc.).
   - I understand the concept of bridging and practice it regularly at work.

Again, the objective here is not to strive for a high score. We want to build around the areas in which we are strong while identifying others that need more work. Take the average score in each group, jot down some reflections, and prioritize your focus going forward.

> *Equitable:* Equitable leaders are committed to and fight for equal access to themselves and other powerful spaces and resources. They naturally share power with their staff and others around them. A few keys to equity are sharing power, providing access into places of power, and pulling others up.

Before we get into a questionnaire, I will provide an example of equitable leadership. Joe was on the leadership team of an organization I was in. Due to Joe's upbringing in a poor neighborhood, he was always committed to using his power to pull less privileged people up. Joe was the type who would teach you to fish instead of fishing for you. He would empower you to try things for yourself so you didn't have to always depend on him.

Whenever a new position opened up, Joe was always thinking about how to either bring in or promote different types of people. If leadership teams were all white, he would question why. Joe was well connected and would bring people into informal spaces to which they might not have access. For example, if Joe was going to meet with the CEO, he would reserve time to address agenda items that people on his radar also had for the CEO. It wasn't about him. Joe was masterful at giving people access to places of power, whether it was within the C-suite, the boardroom, or other spaces that were deemed inaccessible to the average employee.

Joe was an equity icon in my book because access was always on his mind.

Let's Reflect

Based on Joe's example, how far are you away from being equitable on a scale from 1 to 5?

1) Sharing Power
   - I help others access places of power.
   - I share decision making with others who are different from me.
   - I understand what sharing power looks and feels like to others who are different from me.

2) Questioning the Status Quo
   - I regularly question the norms in which we operate.
   - I often audit my team for representation of different voices.
   - I get to the root causes of why certain groups are underrepresented.
   - I refrain from blaming othered folks for their lack of access.

3) Providing Access
   - I bring underrepresented voices into spaces where they are scarce.
   - I provide access to powerful spaces either directly or directly.
   - I challenge others to do the same.
   - I'm not afraid to challenge or break oppressive systems and structures.

Aware: Aware leaders are keen observers and are always monitoring their *below the surface* progress. They know how they are perceived and are always thinking about ways to improve.

Let's discuss Joe's awareness. He would always question his blind spots in any given situation. He also would regularly gather 360 feedback (for development, not performance) and would share his feedback with others, along with his commitments to improve.

Another factor that made Joe exceptionally aware is that he wouldn't get defensive when others provided him with unsolicited feedback. He just listened, even if he didn't agree.

Let's Reflect

Based on Joe's example, how far away are you from being fully aware on a scale of 1 to 5?

1) Checking Biases
   - I often check my bias—specifically, how often I bring the terrible three into my relationships.
     - Affinity Bias
     - Confirmation Bias
     - In-Group Bias
2) Becoming an Observer
   - I allow myself to observe what's really going on.
   - I listen more than I talk.
   - I observe before engaging.
   - I embody observing as a valuable part of listening.
3) Monitoring Self-Awareness
   - I monitor my self-awareness on an ongoing basis.
   - I ask for structured feedback on an ongoing basis.
   - I refrain from defensiveness, even if I don't agree.
   - I am transparent, and share feedback that I receive with others.
   - I take consistent steps to change based on feedback.

Loyal: Loyal leaders create environments for success, failure, and innovation. They lead with psychological safety in mind, create space for mistakes, and provide opportunities for people to redeem themselves. Loyal does not mean that you accept mediocrity. It means you understand that people and progress can be messy and imperfect. In the *below the surface* approach, loyalty is recognized in three ways: seeing things through, accepting imperfections, and sticking things out.

The loyal leader example: Leah promoted me into a new job but when things didn't go as planned during the first year, instead of punishing my performance, she stuck with me. She didn't lose confidence in me. She also shared my mistakes with the team and demonstrated that not only were they expected, they were part of growth.

Let's Reflect

How loyal are you on a scale of 1 to 5?
1) Staying Committed to the Process
   - I am loyal to the *below the surface* process even after making some missteps.
   - I pick up and move on after making a mistake.
   - I trust a process for the long haul, understanding that change does not come quickly.
2) Remaining Healthily Loyal
   - I understand that humans are imperfect and remain healthily loyal.
   - I often give people the benefit of the doubt.

- I don't write someone off for just one mistake.
- I reassure people of my loyalty to them after they experience a setback.

3) Seeing Things Through
   - I stick with people, processes, and things to see them through.
   - I understand that change is a process and treat it as such.
   - I make tweaks instead of starting all over or stopping entirely.
   - I commit to seeing things through even when they don't go as planned the first time.

Calculate your average score for all of these groups of questions and reflect on a couple of factors.

Let's Reflect

1) Which two REAL behaviors would you like to focus more deeply on?
2) What specifically would you like to change?
3) What commitments will you make going forward?

Gain the awareness, make the commitments out loud, and move into practice.

*Note: More extensive tools and questionnaires are available at leadingbelowthesurface.com.

Moving from Learning to Becoming

I've said this several times in this book: The *below the surface* concepts are not complicated. The hardest part is not knowledge; it's going a few steps past that and committing, practicing, and sharing your slips. I'm not going to give you a bunch of actions to take to get there. Becoming is deeper than that. It's gaining awareness and taking tiny steps forward. Becoming is building micro-habits. It's practicing gratitude for every step you take.

In many organizations, the formula to practice goes like this: We learn something and then we take action. But what's missing is embodiment. It's not enough to learn objectively about what a REAL leader is—we have to understand what it feels like when we embody realness. Now that we know what realness is, what does it feel like to embody it?

Let's use relatability as an example. What does being relatable look and feel like to *you*? Is it being a better listener? If so, then start with a micro-habit of putting your phone away when in conversations. Then, move to a micro-habit of playing back what you hear. Keep progressively doing more. Eventually, it won't feel right if you aren't actively listening. You have embodied it. You will instinctively know what the opposite feels like.

This may sound fluffy, but I have seen the alternative, and it doesn't work. We spend so much time trying to control people with formal protocols. We enter a leadership program or take some sort of training, memorize the content, and even try to align our behaviors to "competencies" that we don't believe in. Research says that intrinsic motivation, doing something because you find it motivating, is much more effective than being motivated based on external rewards, like money, attention, etc., in the longer term. So, if you want something to stick, you have to identify and find your own meaning in it.

Yeah, you may need external rewards to form some initial micro-habits, but, in the long run, you have to identify with your own realness and *want* to change for this process to work. This is why I mentioned in Chapter 4 that you don't even have to use the acronym REAL; instead, embody the concepts and find the label that works for you. That's what becoming REAL looks like.

Sharing Your Slips

The last step in becoming a *below the surface leader* is sharing your slips. I recently found myself in a debate about whether, when you are embarking on a new change, you should publicly share your slips with those to whom you communicated the commitment. For example, if you tell your best friend that you are committed to working out five days a week for a month, are you honest with them when you skip a day? Do you share your slip?

If you want to enter into a *below the surface* mindset, sharing your slips is necessary. This isn't the same as shaming or even admitting your failures. Sharing your slips is the process of admitting that none of us are perfect and, as humans, acknowledging that we exclude to belong. Sharing your slips is backing your wholesome goal with full honesty. Nothing is pristine, and the path to truly accessing *below the surface leadership* will be full of slips. Some people even describe slip sharing as spiritual. It's a rebellious level of vulnerability that propels you into deeper levels with others. Sharing your slips is about embodiment, not accomplishment.

Through my work coaching leaders through 360 results, I have found that the most successful leaders are those who share their action plans with their teams and those who balance sharing successes with slips. These same leaders are radically open. They discuss the feedback, how they embodied the feedback, their commitments going forward, and how the team will know they have changed. They share their slips along the way. You can't get more authentic than that, and these are the leaders who experience long-term change.

Summary: Repeat These Steps for Your Entire Career

To recap, the process to become a *below the surface leader* starts with understanding the REAL approach, embodying your own approach, practicing it, and sharing your slips. This process doesn't happen quickly, but you will experience changes over time. Once you understand and embody your realness, it's time to move on to more advanced concepts, such as empathy and psychological safety. As we will explore in Chapter 7, if all else fails, rely on empathy. If you are on a short time frame and want some quick wins before diving into realness, your lifeline is empathy. More on this in the next chapter.

CHAPTER
7

Living on the Edge
with Empathy

The first six chapters of this book focused on the "why" of *below the surface*, and the basics on becoming a *below the surface leader*. I started with why I wrote this book, followed by how to become a *below the surface leader*. We then dug into the REAL approach—learning that *below the surface* leaders are relatable, equitable, aware, and loyal. We also learned that embodying REAL behaviors eventually leads to a change in mindset.

The next couple of chapters are about building depth in relationships. These relationships are your impetus to getting deeper and more settled into *below the surface leadership*. Knowing how difficult navigating surface relationships can be, many of us need a safety valve. A fallback. Something that protects us when we steer off track. Something that is accessible and replicable. Empathy is the *below the surface* fallback.

Empathy as a Reliable *Below the Surface* Fallback

When I was writing this book, I came across a fascinating study led by a few psychologists. They were looking to identify and measure evidence-based ways to reduce racial bias and stereotypes. The study was administered over a 12-week period with undergraduate psychology students.

The students in the experimental group were taught five evidence-based ways to reduce racial bias:

- Stereotype replacement: Recognizing, labeling, and replacing stereotypical behaviors with non-stereotypical responses.
- Counter-stereotypic imaging: Imagining othered folks who are doing things that contradict stereotypical behaviors.
- Individuation: Evaluating someone based on personal attributes as opposed to as a member of an outgroup.
- Perspective taking: Taking the perspective of an othered person, or living in their shoes.
- Increasing opportunities for contact: Finding opportunities to gain exposure to people different from you.

Students were then asked to commit to ways to apply the interventions throughout the study. The participants were told to apply each of these strategies when they found themselves consciously feeling racially biased. Participants also reflected on how they experienced each intervention via a series of questionnaires. Participants' implicit (unconscious) and explicit (conscious) racial bias levels were measured throughout the study to monitor any changes.

The results of the study were remarkable. Participants' implicit biases were notably reduced as measured by the

Implicit Association Tests (IATs) administered throughout the experience. Participants in the experimental group also left the study with more overall concern and awareness around their personal biases. I find this experiment compelling because it suggests that if we apply just one fallback over time, we can transform our entire relationship with bias.[21]

Fallbacks aren't a new concept. Think about the last habit you tried to change or the newest ritual you worked to build. I'm going to use wellness as our example here, as many people can relate. Whether it's diet, exercise, or meditation, we have all been through it. Maybe you wanted to start a new exercise routine or maybe you wanted to practice more mindfulness. On the days where your willpower is working against you, you may need to rely on your fallback to quickly get yourself back on track. For dieting, that fallback might be reverting to your renewed diet the next day; for mindfulness, your fallback might be taking 10 deep breaths in lieu of dedicated sitting time. With exercise, if you skip your planned program, your fallback may be that you at least go walk around the block. You do enough to not lose the habit you have started to build.

The *below the surface* fallback is empathy. What this means is that if everything else fails, practice empathy. It's a *below the surface leader*'s most reliable tool. When you are having a hard day, practice empathy. When you are in doubt, practice empathy. Empathy is essential to *below the surface leadership.* If you get overwhelmed reading this book, practice

---

[21]Patricia Devine et al., "Long-term Reduction in Implicit Race Bias: A Prejudice Habit-Breaking Intervention," *Journal of Experimental Social Psychology* 48, no. 6 (November 2012): 1267–78, https://doi.org/10.1016/j.jesp.2012.06.003.

empathy as a reset. In this chapter, you will learn empathy basics, why it's a *below the surface* fallback, and how to build empathetic rituals to stay on track.

The Basics of Empathy and Active Listening

I discovered the power of empathy first as an employee, and subsequently as a coach. As an employee, true empathy was one of the quickest routes to building trust. All *below the surface* leaders led with empathy first. It was their jam, both as people and as professionals. Although many *below the surface* leaders are natural empaths, empathy is a practice that can be learned. If you feel like you are not great at it, rest assured—you will continue to get better in time.

Empathetic listening is the most accessible way for *below the surface* leaders to access empathy. Listening through an empathetic ear is an extremely powerful connection tool. Research shows that empathetic listening builds trust and respect. Empathetic listening is accessible, in that it is relatively easy to apply and can be accessed in any situation in which you want to quickly connect with people who are different from you, especially with folks who appear not to fit in any given environment.

Before we get into the "how," let's first get on the same page about what empathy is and is not, as there are many misconceptions out there. The way I define empathy is our ability to understand and to connect with the feelings, thoughts, and experiences of others. A tell-tale sign that you are in the room with an empathetic listener is that you immediately have an overwhelming feeling of trust. Empathetic listeners are able to instantly build this trust because they have mastered an essential *below the surface* skill: listening.

It's estimated that less than half of leaders regularly practice empathy.[22] Lack of empathy can be one of the biggest walls standing between you and people different from you. To begin dismantling the wall, you first need to understand what's it's made of.

The Different Types of Listening

In this section, I will focus on two types of listening: surface listening and empathetic (*below the surface*) listening. Most of our interactions are embedded in surface listening. Once you learn about each listening type, we can discuss how to practice them and how to incorporate empathy into all your interactions.

Surface Listening

When you practice surface listening, you are listening with the intent to respond. Unfortunately, most job interviews, routine managerial conversations, and initial "small talk" conversations rely on surface listening. I sometimes refer to surface listening as "selective listening." We are selectively hearing what we want and expect to hear. Our brain is always partially distracted because we are constantly obsessing about our response.

Think about the last transactional conversation you had with someone. You had a goal for the conversation. You likely selectively listened throughout the conversation. You weeded out everything that wasn't important. You probably noticed little about the person with whom you were conversing.

---

[22]Sinar et al., *High Resolution Leadership*, 29.

Surface listening has a necessary place in all of our lives, but all too often, we are listening on a surface level when we should be in *below the surface* listening mode. Any conversation that is transactional requires little emotion, which means it will likely involve surface listening as the primary conversational tactic.

Below the Surface Listening

When we are practicing *below the surface* listening, we are fully tuned into our interactions. Two different types of *below the surface* listening help you tap into empathy: person-to-person listening and person-to-belonging listening.

Person-to-Person (P2P) Listening

P2P listening involves engaging on a deeper level and with multiple senses, including sight, smell, and even the sixth sense—intuition. *Below the surface P2P interpersonal listening* is amongst the most essential and reliable resources when building relationships with people who are different from you. *Below the surface* P2P listening is powerful because when we do it well, people immediately feel seen and heard. They instantly open up, so you can quickly generate a sense of connection. When we are listening in a *below the surface* sense, we are zooming in on the person via multiple senses.

Some other basics of P2P listening:

a) You are practicing active listening techniques. This involves asking open-ended questions, checking for understanding, and summarizing interactions.

b) You are spending the vast majority of time listening, not talking. When you are talking, it's mainly to check for understanding.

c) You don't notice anything else in the room except for you and the other person.

d) You are cycling through and playing things back, checking for understanding. You are curious and you continue to reflect.

This is not a transaction. You are genuinely connecting with the person.

In your next few conversations, take the opportunity to practice P2P listening. You don't need to limit yourself to practicing with people who are different from you. The goal is to start to build a habit around P2P listening to the point that it becomes natural and you can immediately recognize if you are at a surface or *below the surface* level with a person.

A quick warning: While P2P listening sounds like common sense, practicing it does not come easily for many of us. Our worlds are full of distractions. We are always on standby, checking our phones and wanting people to speed up their communication and cut to the chase. It takes some time to train your brain out of this. However, when you look at the research, empathy is indeed a very reliable (and accessible) recourse.

If you find yourself attempting to practice P2P listening and are struggling, here are four go-to actions you can try out to stay the course during your first few conversations:

1) **Use power-sharing tactics to open the conversation.** If there is a power differential between you and the person you are interacting with, this step is especially

important. You want to level the playing field for your interaction. You can't see the world from another person's perspective if you are on a higher stoop than them. Some ways to level the power fields:

a) Convene in a neutral spot when possible.
b) Approach them; don't wait for them to approach you.
c) Physically put yourself on equal ground as them (if they are sitting, you sit too).
d) Ask for permission early and often (like, "do you mind if I join you?" instead of just infiltrating someone's space).

There are certainly more advanced power sharing tactics, but these four will help you get started.

2) **Stay in playback mode.** One of the easiest ways to stay 100% in a conversation is to settle in "playback mode." In playback mode, we repeat words, tones, and body language movements that we have observed. We essentially run these observations by the other person to make sure that we are accurately understanding them. The easiest way to stay in a conversation is to play back what the person is saying in your head while they are talking. Do the same out loud once they pause. You can also play back emotions or feelings. Example: "I noticed your voice changed when you said _____. It sounds like you're very excited about it." Also, ask someone what you may have missed to continue leveling the power field.

3) **Observe and deliver ongoing conversation cues.** Another way to stay focused in *below the surface* P2P communications is to provide ongoing conversation and feedback

cues. Your feedback can be in the form of body or verbal language. For example, you can nod your head, smile, or say things such as, "That's a great point," or "I noticed that we didn't connect as deeply on _____."

4) **Enter the conversation with intention.** If you are having a tough time staying in *below the surface* communication, try to get settled in your intentions before your conversation starts. You can do this by taking 10 deep breaths. You will slow yourself down immediately. Also, write down any outdated conversational habits you want to discontinue. Setting your pace in intention will go a long way, especially in those first few conversations.

Below the surface P2P listening techniques can be used in basically any conversation but are especially useful to get you on a fast track to empathy. Once you step back and are actually hearing someone, you can begin to understand their perspective. People, especially those who are different from us, often walk away from conversations feeling misunderstood. As leaders, we are often not 100% present. Assumptions take over because we don't have the patience or attention span to truly sit in a conversation. Try P2P listening with everyone for a week and do some journaling on it. Remember, real relationships take time, patience, and investment. While this isn't exactly rocket science, it also isn't instinctual or simple. The key is practicing and actually sitting down to do it so you get a good dose of what P2P feels like, and to begin building new habits that incorporate P2P listening in all of your interactions. You need to build a P2P habit to get deep and start to build trust.

Person-to-Belonging (P2B) Listening

Once you have practiced *below the surface* P2P listening, you will start to build the confidence and competence to move into *below the surface* person-to-belonging listening. *Below the surface P2B listening* takes P2P listening one step deeper. *Below the surface* P2B listening is another accessible and reliable route to building empathy and trust. In *below the surface* P2B listening, you become an observer and start seeing others as part of a larger environment. Observing becomes your most powerful tactic. You are listening in a compound fashion and are able to dually explore the person and the environment that the person is in.

Examples of P2B listening include discerning when someone doesn't quite fit into an environment, observing when someone seems out of sorts, and seeing how organizational systems may be marginalizing folks. P2B listening is difficult to do without first practicing P2P listening. You can't notice or observe how someone is fitting into an environment until you have actually engaged them in empathetic listening. Also, a basic level of trust is necessary to effectively navigate P2B listening.

I'm going to use a personal example to describe P2B listening, and why it is a prerequisite. The first time I experienced P2B listening was well into my professional career. I had been hired by a firm to expand their competency in a highly demanded client area. Early on, I realized that I didn't fit into the firm. Most of the people went to the same schools and were recruited on campus, so there was a Greek organization, college party-type camaraderie. I was also older and more experienced than many of my colleagues. These factors instantly made me feel othered.

The leader who hired me, Rich, ran the entire practice. Invested in my success, he enlisted several mentors for me. He also gave me open access to him. I could call him anytime, and when he didn't answer, he found a minute to call me back in a timely manner. My relationship with Rich was the only thing that kept me at the firm, but that didn't change my day-to-day experience of not fitting in. There was one particular experience that highlighted the extent to which that was the case.

When I was staffed with a large client, our contract ended up getting extended—mainly due to efforts made by myself and a colleague. The firm held a large celebration designed to honor both of us, but the whole thing was too much for me. The lavish event felt like it crossed the line. The pool party seemed extra. I felt uncomfortable, so I left the party. I didn't realize that Rich saw me leave.

The following week, I had a 1:1 with Rich. We met in a neutral place, and Rich started the conversation off with P2P listening. This is why I had complete trust in Rich. He always listened to me and followed through with his commitments. I knew he was listening to me as he also tied references from past conversations to current ones.

After some small talk about the weather, Rich asked me a few questions:

How was I doing?
How were my last few weeks?
What could the firm do better?

After each question, he played back my words and emotions. For example, when asked how I was doing, he acknowledged that I seemed overwhelmed. I confirmed my feelings of burnout.

Rich took the conversation a notch deeper:

Rich: Something seems off. You seem a little more short with me than usual. What are you not saying right now?

That's when I started to open up:

Me: Yeah, I really appreciate the celebration but I didn't feel like I fit in there.

Rich: Oh, that makes sense. I've noticed that you have left a number of social events early. It looks like you aren't having fun at all. What is it?

Me: I'm not. These parties aren't my idea of fun. I felt bad as I knew the party was for me. I'm feeling out of place at pretty much every social event.

Rich: Well, if you're feeling this way, I'm sure others are as well. Maybe, we can put a committee together to explore how we can celebrate in ways that work for everyone.

Me: That would be great. Perhaps we can do something meaningful like volunteering or maybe even something active.

Rich: I agree. We never explored that.

Rich was engaging with me on a P2B level. Before that conversation, I had never experienced an approach like this. Rich "saw" me, even at times when I didn't think he did. Discernment played a big role. Rich was a great P2B *listener*. He was a keen observer and took time to really see what was going on. Most leaders are racing through their day, so to know that Rich was actually taking the time to listen and observe what I was going through cemented our relationship.

As you can see from Rich's example, *below the surface* P2B listening involves listening with multiple senses. P2B listeners are keen observers. It's virtually impossible to be able to listen on a P2B level if you haven't engaged with that same person already in several P2P conversations. It's because P2P listening builds the requisite trust you need to get deeper with others.

Now, it's your turn. Let's practice P2B listening.

Let's Try This

In all your interactions over the next few weeks, try to spend more time observing and listening rather than talking. Notice how people who are different from you are experiencing the world. Observe—and ask—what's happening in their bodies. Sit back and absorb all the things that you were missing before you started practicing *below the surface* listening.

Summary: The Relationship Between Empathy and *Below the Surface* Listening

This chapter is about relying on empathy as a fallback *below the surface* action. When nothing else is available, rely on empathy.

There are two types of *below the surface* listening: 1) active listening, or *person-to-person (P2P) listening*, and 2) listening to understand the extent in which a person belongs in their environment, or *person-to-belonging (P2B) listening*. Both types of listening are important to access empathy. P2P listening allows you to plant the seeds for real relationships through active, engaged listening. Such listening leads to trust over time. P2B listening takes P2P listening one step forward. Once you have the relationship, you can start to observe people (especially those who are different from you) to discern the extent to which they belong in an environment. P2B listening is better relied on when the relationship is already established.

In P2B listening, share your observations and confirm them. For example:

> I noticed that . . .
> It seems like . . .
> It appears that . . .

Playing statements back, in a way that is inquisitive and checks for understanding and confirmation, is what active listening is all about: listening to understand. If you put that front and center, you will be just fine consistently accessing empathy.

But there's more. In Chapter 8, we will learn about psychological safety and how practicing *below the surface* listening leads us into psychologically safe relationships.

Moving Into Psychologically Safe Relationships

At one point in my career, I was matched with the best mentor I ever had. Linda could do no wrong and it seemed like she could walk on water. Linda had a great deal of power and influence in our organization. She used that power to open doors for me, providing me access to incredible developmental opportunities. Linda seemed to get everything that she wanted; she was also extremely bold. She made unorthodox decisions, but the company never vetoed any of them. Linda had some wins and losses, but her reputation never suffered. She demonstrated what my colleagues and I called "protected people." Protected people were almost always folks from the core group. Their ticket to entry was that they first had to look and feel like everyone else. Then, with each rung they climbed, they acquired more and more keys to powerful spaces. After a while, they were invincible.

Protected folks seemed to earn a premium tag at some point very early in their career. For some, it didn't take much.

As long as you either had connections, looked or felt like the core group, or accomplished something revered by the core group, you were *in*. Once you were in, you stayed in. Your career was set. This is what made Linda the best mentor I ever had. She had this indestructible power, and she used it to pull me up. I tried to replicate Linda's formula for success in my career, but it never worked. There was no rhyme or reason to consistently breaking into the core. Linda made it look easy. I tried twice as hard, but it became too draining to continue. The system wasn't made for me.

It wasn't until many years later that I learned the academic word for Linda's situation. Among other things, Linda had psychological safety, and a great deal of it. That psychological safety enabled her to do her best work while bringing her entire self to the office. According to Amy C. Edmondson in *The Fearless Organization*:

> Psychological safety is broadly defined as a climate in which people are comfortable expressing themselves. They are confident that they can speak up and won't be humiliated, ignored, or blamed. When a work environment has reasonably high psychological safety, good things happen: mistakes are reported quickly so that prompt corrective action can be taken, seamless coordination across groups or departments is enabled, and potentially game-changing ideas for innovation are shared.[23]

[23]Amy C. Edmondson, *The Fearless Organization: Creating Psychological Safety in the Workplace for Learning, Innovation and Growth* (Hoboken, NJ: John Wiley & Sons, 2019), loc. 357, Kindle.

In addition to improved trust, psychological safety has been tied to increased confidence, creativity, and productivity.[24] People who experience psychological safety can more easily live in their purpose while bringing their entire selves to work. Psychological safety has also been tied to higher employee engagement. People intrinsically are more connected to their work when they have a heightened sense of belonging.

Edmondson noted that you can gauge psychological safety by measuring the extent to which:

- Mistakes are not held against you.
- Team members are encouraged to bring up problems and tough issues.
- People on the team are not rejected for being different.
- It's safe to take risks.
- People can feel comfortable asking for help.
- People don't undermine each other; and
- People's unique skills and talents are valued and utilized.[25]

The way Linda was treated at work was aligned to all seven measures. Linda's ideas were never ignored, and departments across the organization were on board with Linda's company-proclaimed brilliance. As I watched Linda, it was as if her ideas were better because of all the positive reinforcement. Linda appeared as if she knew she was protected, which emboldened her to put her best and brightest ideas out there. She was one of the only women on the leadership team,

[24]Yanfei Wang, Jieqiong Liu, and Yu Zhu, "Humble Leadership, Psychological Safety, Knowledge Sharing, and Follower Creativity: A Cross-Level Investigation," *Frontiers in Psychology* 9 (September 2018): 1727, https://doi.org/10.3389/fpsyg.2018.01727.

[25]Edmondson, *The Fearless Organization*.

and that difference was respected. Linda brought ideas to the table that nobody else had. She had built up so much armor that even if people did try to undermine her, they didn't get far. Linda truly brought her entire self to work every day. She knew that she was an integral part of the organization. What a great feeling to have at work.

True Psychological Safety is Uncommon, Especially for Othered Folks

Psychological safety is an uncommon feeling to experience in the workplace. As referenced in Chapter 5, according to Gallup, only 30% of employees feel that their opinions count at work.[26] This is an alarming statistic. Let's unpack this for a second. Imagine that you are on a team of 10. According to this Gallup statistic, only three people's opinions on the team count. Think about the last time you were on a team of 10. Is this consistent with your experience? When we consider it from that angle, it may not be surprising at all.

When I was in business school, I was assigned to multiple teams throughout the year. I realized that I only felt safe on one or two of those teams, out of about a dozen or more. So, these statistics make sense. On those teams, usually one or two people would take over and only ask for input from those they liked. I was relegated to othered status very quickly.

This made me speculate that since psychological safety is unlikely for everyone, it must be a pipe dream for folks on the margins. Unfortunately, there isn't much research out there

---

[26] *Employee Engagement and Performance: Latest Insights From the World's Largest Study* (Gallup, 2020) https://www.gallup.com/workplace/321032/employeeengagement-meta-analysis-brief.aspx.

that shows the relationship between othered folks and psychological safety. However, I would argue that considering the unique challenges we face in the workplace, the situation is even more dire for us. I'm basing this position on personal experiences, client experiences, and statistics about othered folks at work. I'm going to provide examples of each.

First off, consider these statistics:

- 50% of LGBTQ+ folks still elect to stay in the closet due to fear of being penalized at work.[27]
- 37% of othered folks reported that they left their jobs due to unfair treatment at work.[28]
- 25% of othered folks reported experiencing stereotyping at work.[29]
- On average, Black employees tend to feel unsafe opening up to white employees because they feel that information would be used against them.[30]
- Almost half of Black employees in the workplace have experienced blatant racism.[31]

---

[27]*A Workplace Divided: Understanding the Climate for LGBTQ Workers Nationwide* (Human Rights Campaign, 2018) https://www.hrc.org/resources/a-workplace-divided-understanding-the-climate-for-lgbtq-workers-nationwide.

[28]Scott, Klein, and Onovakpuri, *Tech Leavers Study.*

[29]Scott, Klein, and Onovakpuri, *Tech Leavers Study.*

[30]Katherine W. Phillips, Tracy L. Dumas, and Nancy P. Rothbard, "Diversity and Authenticity," *Harvard Business Review*, March–April 2018, https://hbr.org/2018/03/diversity-and-authenticity.

[31]"Glassdoor Survey Finds Three in Five U.S. Employees Have Experienced or Witnessed Distrimination Based on Age, Race, Gender or LGBTQ at Work," Glassdoor, October 23, 2019, https://about-content.glassdoor.com/en-us/diversity-inclusion-2019/.

The statistics suggest that psychological safety is merely a fantasy in many organizations, and the chances of achieving it are even more dire for marginalized folks. This is the very definition of othering; you exist on the outskirts. The basics aren't even being tended to for othered folks. Sometimes you aren't even receiving cursory respect at work. Even if you are a moderately successful other, you still rarely feel like you can bring your entire self to work.

There were only two jobs in my career where I felt 100% psychologically safe. This was achieved because I was not only supported by my manager but also by my manager's manager. The latter was high up enough to influence their peers, too. It was like a small invisible village surrounding and protecting me. They went out and scouted for my food and water. They taught me how to fish instead of doing it for me. They didn't want me to experience any malevolent behavior. They taught me everything I needed to know in order to thrive. It was and is an amazing feeling. Granted, not everyone will always like you, but the people who matter do. Even though I experienced some safety, I never did to the extent that Linda did. She was invincible.

My clients—especially othered folks—also have similar experiences. Like me, they also struggle to achieve psychological safety at work. Let's take the story of Carmine, a young, rising Black female executive. Carmine's story is the story of many of my clients. The CEO of XYZ Tech hired Carmine to be the company's head of finance. Carmine was more than qualified for the job but learned shortly after she was hired that there had been an internal male colleague from XYZ Tech's core group who had unsuccessfully applied for the role. Carmine didn't want to let that slow her down. The CEO had hired her and she was excited to make an impact in her first C-suite role. She wrote the whole situation off as superficial gossip.

The first few months went well for Carmine. Her peers were being really "nice" to her. I am specifically calling that out, as they were more *polite* than *helpful*. Carmine noticed this right away. The CEO had asked them to welcome her to her new position. Carmine cautiously accepted their niceness as she had a ton to learn. Once Carmine learned the ropes, she focused on building a team. She also spent time building relationships with her newly formed team. That was difficult, considering the internal circumstances, but after a few months of persistent and consistent 1:1s, Carmine felt like her team was functioning well. About six months in, the company was going through a fundraising process, and Carmine was tapped by the CEO to help lead the efforts. The task was that she take on a co-lead role to get the entire C-suite aligned and organized.

The process was going very fast, so Carmine needed her peers to be responsive and supportive. But the nice behavior suddenly stopped. Carmine's peers started to complain to the CEO that she was being too aggressive. Her colleagues had a specific way of communicating, and Carmine didn't conform to that. They called her a "bulldog" since, instead of asking about sports or having small talk before stating her purpose for a meeting, Carmine cut right to the chase. This was Carmine's style. It had always been that way.

Carmine had been quickly relegated to an other. Because she was a Black woman, this didn't take long. They didn't like her. She didn't fit in. She wasn't part of the core group. When the CEO brought this feedback to her attention, Carmine made some adjustments. Sports weren't an interest for her, so she tried to find other things to connect on. Although

Carmine attempted to practice compassion with her peers, the situation only got worse. Soon, all of Carmine's peers were complaining about her. The CEO was complicit and asked for her to handle it. Although he said he still supported her, his actions proved otherwise.

Carmine ended up leaving that job after eight months. She was exhausted. Psychological safety was rampantly lacking for her. When she hired me as a coach, she was looking to turn it around, but quickly realized that she was at a point of no return at XYZ Tech. We found her a new opportunity in which psychological safety was front and center. She asked tough questions as she didn't want to repeat the same situation.

I'm sure that Carmine's story isn't much different from those you know. Most of us lack psychological safety at work, but for othered folks, the situation is much more dire. While lack of *below the surface leadership* is a factor, there are also many more processes that contribute to a dearth of psychological safety in organizations. These are usually foundational processes that corporations build themselves on.

What's Standing in Your Way? Top *Below the Surface* Psychological Safety Roadblocks

So many organizations struggle with psychological safety because their foundational talent practices are the antithesis of it. Numerous practices perpetuate it. I'm going to focus on four in the next section: Suppressive Corporate Talent Processes, the Terrible Three, Underestimating Basic Human Needs, and the Myth of the Manager.

Suppressive Corporate Talent Processes

Corporate Talent Processes include full-cycle talent management functions ranging from hiring to employee engagement. While *all* of these processes can squelch psychological safety in organizations, I'm going to focus on the most pervasive one: performance management.

I've worked with countless companies that bragged that they had the best performance management in the world. This translated to the fact that they had pay-for-performance programs. They also believed they had a meritocracy and rewarded the best employees with the biggest raises based on their individual abilities and efforts.

Meritocracies grew in popularity during the Jack Welch era at General Electric (GE) in the 1990s. Many organizations jumped on the bandwagon as they figured that was their ticket to building a high-performing culture. My main issue with meritocracies has always been that you have to compete with peers, sometimes those with entirely different talents. In many cases, you have no chance. And it becomes about surface things, not your actual performance. For more transaction-based careers, some aspects of a meritocracy could work. One could be reasonably successful arguing for a meritocracy for sales folks or any other transactional group that is clearly measured by numbers. But even then, there could be bias in the system. So, for most organizations, we should stay away from meritocracy and science tells us why.

In one particular study, Emilio Castilla, a researcher at Massachusetts Institute of Technology (MIT), examined a company with almost 9,000 employees. According to mainstream standards, the organization would have been considered a high-performing company. It heavily invested in its employees, innovation, and the general organization. It also prided itself on its meritocracy.[32]

Castilla found that bias ran rampant in this particular meritocracy. Although this company claimed to reward employees fairly, based on ability and effort, Castilla's findings proved otherwise. He found that, despite earning similar performance ratings, othered folks—including women, BIPOC folks, and non-U.S.-based employees—received smaller increases in compensation compared with white men in the performance process. Even though it was a "pay-for-performance culture," the othered folks needed to "work harder and obtain higher performance scores in order to receive similar salary increases to white men."[33]

Meritocracies have also been linked to more selfish, ultra-competitive behaviors. Think dog-eat-dog environments. When trying to have a leg up over someone, you are defying the very definition of psychological safety by undermining one another. I experienced this both in corporate HR and as an employee. Instead of competing against yourself and the goals you set, you're put up against your peers. This causes a culture of competition that makes psychological safety even harder to come by. In many of these companies, it's not about making the workplace safer for colleagues; it becomes about being better than them. Conniving behaviors follow, and this brings out the opposite of what safety is meant to be.

There are many more talent processes stifling psychological safety but performance management is the most

---

[32]Emilio J. Castilla, "Gender, Race, and Meritocracy in Organizational Careers," *American Journal of Sociology* 113, no. 6 (May 2008): 1479–526, https://doi.org/10.1086/588738.

[33]Marianne Cooper, "The False Promise of Meritocracy," *The Atlantic*, December 1, 2015, https://www.theatlantic.com/business/archive/2015/12/meritocracy/418074/.

notorious. In many companies, it's considered a foundational organizational process—but so many of us have it all wrong.

The Terrible Three

In Chapter 3, I discussed the factious three biases that humans fall into when they are striving to belong. These include affinity bias, confirmation bias, and in-group bias. We tend to conform rather than rely on individual judgment, we naturally hold others who are similar to us in a more positive light, we tend to think we have people all figured out, and we tend to hold people in higher regard when they are part of our own in-group. All of the behaviors in the terrible three hold us back from creating psychological safety, particularly with people who are different from us. We tend to give folks who are similar to us the benefit of the doubt. We also tend to emulate the behaviors of others around us. If we observe that others are being pushed to the margins, then we might do the same thing as we exclude to belong.

Underestimating Basic Human Needs

In order to attain psychological safety, we first need to tend to basic human needs. This is one of the biggest roadblocks out there, but it's a consideration that many organizations overlook. I often have potential clients reach out because they want to create cultures of belonging, and psychological safety is proposed to be the foundation of the engagement. Sometimes, I outright have to turn potential clients down as it's clear that they haven't tended to the basic needs of their employees. When I say basic needs, I mean living wages, basic respect, physical safety, and other foundational qualities. You can't attain psychological safety if basic needs are not being met.

I usually tell these types of potential clients to reach out when their organizations provide the basics, and we can work on psychological safety once folks are paid what they are worth. Think of it as Maslow's hierarchy of needs. Basic survival needs have to be met before you can move to psychological safety.

The Myth of the Manager

"People leave managers, not companies." My bosses would say this over and over throughout my career. This saying is based on studies that have been done over the years. I reviewed some of these studies and tested this assertion. My anecdotal results—while it is clear that good managers are *a* reason why people stay at their jobs, they may not be *the* reason.

When it comes to psychological safety, managers are only the start of it. I have had numerous clients leave jobs not because of a lack of psychological safety with their manager but because they lacked support outside of their manager. I've even had that happen to me personally. Psychological safety is not a one-person job. It starts with your manager, but the entire team also has to be aligned if we truly want to create psychological safety. The chronic issue is that organizations pour a ton of money into making managers better. This is shortsighted as it may start there, but it certainly doesn't end there. They are frivolously throwing away money at only part of the problem.

How to Move to Psychologically Safe Relationships

Now that you know psychological safety is lacking in the workplace, let's move to what you can do to promote it. There are three steps you can take to turn things around:

1) Infuse Empathetic Listening into Daily Leadership Habits.
2) Practice P2B Listening.
3) Subvert Poisonous Organizational Systems.

Infuse Empathetic Listening into Daily Leadership Habits

An accessible way to create psychological safety in the workplace is to infuse empathy in your everyday leadership practices. In Chapter 7, we dug deep into empathetic listening and *how* to do it. Achieving psychological safety is another reason *why* you should do it. Empathetic listening brings us closer to building psychological safety with others as it provides an opening to build real relationships with people who are different from us. We learn about how they want to contribute at work and what their unique talents and skills are—and most importantly, we show them that we value them as we authentically listen and follow through on our commitments.

Remember Carmine, the executive I mentioned earlier? Well, Carmine went on to work for a company that practiced empathetic listening from the beginning before she was even hired. She entered her new role with psychological safety. Here's how.

Carmine initially learned about this new role through a connection she met at a conference, Rosa. Rosa was on a competitor's leadership team, and Carmine built a relationship with her over time. Rosa was always a good listener and, through multiple conversations, made Carmine realize that she wasn't doing anything wrong; she was simply in the wrong place. Carmine didn't *only* vent to Rosa. It was deeper than that. Rosa listened to Carmine, boosted her confidence, and renewed her sense of belonging as an executive. When a position opened at Rosa's company, the first person she called was Carmine. When she learned that Carmine was interested, Rosa immediately talked to her CEO and shared Carmine's entire situation with him. Since Carmine was only with XYZ Tech for a short time, she wanted to dissolve any red flags that came up.

Working from Rosa's referral, the CEO ended up quickly interviewing Carmine. He reassured her that he understood why she was leaving XYZ Tech so quickly and that the situation would not be replicated at this job. The CEO was able to get to this place with her as he was capable of listening to Carmine, understanding her talents, and not holding her past mistakes against her in the conversation. He didn't interrogate her or let her past define her.

This is what infusing empathetic listening into your daily habits looks like. Both Rosa and her CEO were capable of empathetically listening to Carmine. Through this listening, they were able to create instant psychological safety for Carmine. This was deeper than the "niceness" that Carmine experienced at XYZ Tech. It was on a different level. It was psychological safety. You know you have it when it's present.

Practice P2B Listening

Practicing P2B listening is another way to progressively move towards psychological safety. This concept was discussed in detail in Chapter 7. P2B listening is environmental listening; it goes beyond the person. You are also attentive to seeing what is going on around the person. You observe the extent to which they fit into the environment. P2B listening is useful in creating psychological safety. It acts as your compass. If you are adept at observing, you can see who is penalized for making mistakes, who is not actively involved in discussions, and who seems to be holding back.

Think of it this way: You access relationships with P2P listening and deepen relationships with P2B listening. It's useful to tap into P2B listening throughout the relationship. This allows you to continuously deepen interactions and consistently move towards psychological safety.

Subvert Poisonous Organizational Systems (If You Can't Dismantle Them Entirely)

As discussed earlier in this chapter, many talent management processes in organizations actively operate in opposition to psychologically safety. Another way to move to more psychologically safe relationships is to actively dismantle those systems. Instead of expecting employees to compete with their colleagues, expect them to compete with themselves. Review the science behind your processes to make sure that what you are doing actually works and is backed by scientific data. For example, science found long ago that pay-for-performance and meritocracies don't work. So why are organizations still building around them?

I realize that many of us may not be in the position to change entire talent processes, so my motto is, "If you can't change it, subvert it." For example, if you are a manager or in a position of power, make small shifts on your team to subvert pervasive organizational talent processes. Comply with performance management, but go one step further on your team and practice authentic career development with your staff. Get to know your staff on a *below the surface* level for healthy, productive relationships. Compliance with the performance process doesn't have to stifle your *below the surface* behavior. You can do the same as an individual contributor. Share the concepts with your team so you can develop your own culture. Change what's in front of you first.

Summary: Psychological Safety Recap

We have now gone over psychological safety and how important it is in truly building real relationships. Psychological safety is an output of empathetic listening. It can be blocked by Suppressive Corporate Talent Processes, the Terrible Three, Underestimating Basic Human Needs, and the Myth of the Manager. Psychologically safe relationships are built by infusing empathetic listening into daily leadership habits, practicing P2B listening, and subverting poisonous organizational systems. In Chapter 9, I will shift to a more broad application of *below the surface* concepts. I will also answer a question that I often get: How do I create a *below the surface* culture?

PART III

Applying the *Below the Surface* Approach in Your Organization

Building a *Below the Surface* Culture

How do you build a *below the surface* culture? I get this question a lot, and what people are truly asking me to address is:

- How do we create a culture of belonging?
- How do we ensure that equity is a part of it?
- Why do culture initiatives never seem to truly stick?

The answer lies in first accessing the deepest levels of your culture. In this chapter, we will discuss culture fundamentals, the three levels of culture, and how to get *below the culture surface* in your organization. We will also discuss how to activate the power that we all have to change our cultures.

A Quick Background on Organizational Culture

What exactly is culture? It's important to answer this question before diving into this chapter as, based on both research and my experience with coaching organizations, culture is one of the most misaligned organizational structures out there.

I spent a decent amount of time in large corporations, managing talent functions, and the culture groundswell started in the mid-2000s. Around that time is when you saw a ubiquitous company culture obsession. "Culture" quickly blossomed into the hottest HR trend. Startups instantly latched onto the promise of hedonistic work environments and even started grandstanding about their "great cultures."

Soon, these same organizations started boasting about their "cultures of fun." I was confused, as I didn't really know what that meant. Fun is a social construct. It means different things to different people, so what exactly was the driver of the fun? As someone who had never worked for a company that I would have described as "fun," I was very skeptical and intrigued at the same time. My curiosity was through the roof.

I started studying, chatting with, and even interviewing these "great culture" companies. I was deeply intrigued by the promise of being happy at work. Of bringing my dog to work. Of bringing my full self to work. Of escaping all of the office eyesores of corporate America. Of having fun. I was fooled by what I call the *great culture lie*. I soon learned firsthand that it was all a scam—a scam no different from the cheap ads you see on the internet. This one is simply less taboo. It has become normal to deceive people.

In my epic quest for work happiness, I decided to interview with one of these "great culture" tech companies, but it left a bad taste in my mouth. The company headhunted me and wanted to discuss a new role that seemed perfectly suited and created for my skill set. I flew across the country to interview with this company, Surface, Inc. My willingness to commute thousands of miles shows the extent to which I was buying up every share of what they were selling, and at premium rates. I was willing to commute across the country because I was needy and quickly obsessed with the great culture lie.

Things turned quickly. I instantly realized that they were the same as everyone else. When I arrived at the interview, I was looked up and down with confusion. It was almost as if they expected me to look or dress differently. I was then escorted to the person who would be my boss, and he walked me over to the office cafe to have lunch. We probably spent about 45 minutes together and I would say that he was only truly present for five minutes of that time, specifically when he shared the menu with me. His body language showed me how tremendously uncomfortable with and disinterested in me he was.

After lunch, he checked the obligatory "company tour" box. The first place he took me was the "fun room," which was completely *empty*. Not a soul. What happened to all the fun rooms overflowing with socializing employees? Especially during lunch hour? I thought that was a little off. Not one person was shooting pool or playing ping-pong.

Long story short, I proceeded through the rest of an interview process with mixed reception. Some interviewers clamored about my skill set and how useful it would be to the company. Others complained about my would-be boss the entire time. The red flags were there, but I still held out hope. Maybe it was an off-hour for the fun room? Maybe my would-be boss was having a bad day? Maybe he was just being negative? I was in denial.

A week later, I received a rejection voicemail—*voicemail*—from Surface, Inc. They weren't such a "great culture" after all. I spent eight weeks talking to this company, and this is all I get? The great culture lie strikes again. You couldn't even have a conversation with me? Not surprising, especially if you can't make eye contact.

Culture Essentials that Organizations Frequently Miss

While Surface, Inc.'s behavior was devastating at the time, the situation also inspired my quest to truly understand culture. What was it really? Is there actually such a thing as a "great culture?" I read dozens of books and papers. One of the first authors I studied was Edgar Schein. I soon learned that Schein was often referred to as the "godfather of culture," so I disproportionately dug into his work. In Schein's model, culture is defined as:

> A pattern of shared basic assumptions that the group learned as it solved its problems of external adaptation and internal integration, that has worked well enough to be considered valid and, therefore, to be taught to new members as the correct way to perceive, think, and feel in relation to those problems."[34]

For comparison sake, here is another more recent example, according to *Harvard Business Review* (*HBR*), written in a different tone:

---

[34]Edgar H. Schein, "Coming to a New Awareness of Organizational Culture," *MIT Sloan Management Review* 25, no. 2 (Winter 1984): 3–16, https://sloanreview.mit.edu/article/coming-to-a-new-awareness-of-organizational-culture.

Culture is the tacit social order of an organization: It shapes attitudes and behaviors in wide-ranging and durable ways. Cultural norms define what is encouraged, discouraged, accepted, or rejected within a group. When properly aligned with personal values, drives, and needs, culture can unleash tremendous amounts of energy toward a shared purpose and foster an organization's capacity to thrive.[35]

There are clear underlying fundamentals in both of these definitions. First off, as stated in both, culture is shared. People are either constantly co-creating ways of operating and/or are constantly told and reinforced how to act. In other words, culture can be shared through co-creation or imposition. The second fundamental is that culture is tacit, meaning if we are on autopilot, then that state of autopilot becomes our culture whether we name it or not.

Through exploring these fundamentals, it's clear that we have to first understand our assumptions and natural ways of being to access what our culture even is. Going below the culture surface is a must. Culture is very difficult for organizations to access, which is the exact reason why so many fail in the culture realm. They fail to get *below the surface* and to mine their daily actions—the actions on which their very culture is built, whether they like it or not.

This is why it's very difficult to develop a culture of belonging. Organizations are focused on the wrong actions. They are throwing surface solutions at a *below the surface* problem. There is no such thing as a great culture. Great

---

[35]Boris Groysberg et al., "The Leader's Guide to Corporate Culture," *Harvard Business Review*, January–February 2018, https://hbr.org/2018/01/the-leaders-guide-to-corporate-culture.

culture for whom? Great culture for what? Calling something a "great culture" doesn't mean anything. Before you can even describe your culture, you first must ask yourself if it's surface or not. If your culture is surface, then you don't have much of one.

You can't truly understand, mold, or change your culture if you are operating at a surface level. This might sound daunting, but getting *below the surface* is only the *beginning* of the journey.

Getting Below the Culture Surface

As I stated earlier, you can't build a culture of belonging unless you are willing to get below the culture surface. You have to go to uncomfortable places and stay there for long periods of time. You have to regularly take steps back and evaluate whether or not your actions align with your culture. It can be challenging to go deep—it's commonly difficult to get to those areas because we may not know that those areas are important, we may not have the right equipment, or going deep may simply be undesirable to surface leaders.

Getting *below the surface* as a leader and getting below the culture surface follow similar approaches, so let's flashback to Chapter 4. As discussed, getting *below the surface* is difficult; it's like getting to the deepest levels of the ocean. As we get further and further down into the ocean, visibility becomes increasingly cloudy and the environment becomes more and more obscure. We know little about ocean life at the deepest levels.

Our relationships with our organizations are parallel to our relationship with the ocean. We tend to stick at the shallowest level and rarely do we access the deepest levels.

We may not realize the need to go there, or maybe we don't know how to get there. Like many organizations, perhaps we want to stick to the shallowest levels in order to reap the superficial benefits. Perhaps we are afraid of the ominous environment we may encounter at the deepest levels. But the deeper in the organization you get, the more you can truly understand, connect to, discern, and shape it.

The Below the Culture Surface Levels Explained

Consistent with *below the surface leadership* levels, the three levels of culture are: *surface level, transitional level,* and the *below the surface level.* The surface level is the entry level of culture. When organizations know they need to take action on their culture, they start here, and many end here. In the middle we have the transitional level, and the deepest level is the *below the surface* level—below the culture surface.

The Culture Surface Level

The shallowest level of culture is at the surface. The *surface level* is what you see when you walk into an organization, go on their website, or even when you interact with their leaders. Like in the ocean, it's the level that's the most frequented— the one we can see and access, and subsequently know the most about. It's the more outward-facing aspects of an organization. Tangibles reside on the surface level. They are things that we can see and touch. In Shein's theory, he refers to visible culture objects as artifacts; these include websites, press, and even office design and decor. Surface cultures are performative in that they are 100% focused on surface artifacts.

They look pretty on paper but there's nothing more beyond that. It is comfortable to exist at shallow levels.

I have functioned within many surface cultures, but there's one in particular that has always stuck with me. The company, job, pay, and benefits were great. When I was hired, the company also bragged about its amazing culture. It basically said that everyone could bring their entire selves to work. To my dismay, I saw on the very first day that that wasn't true. My manager was terrible. She scolded us in public and didn't trust our team. She challenged the time off I took when I lost a close family member. I was living the great culture lie. *The surface culture was great, but the company was stuck there.* I left at the first chance I got.

The Culture Transitional Level

The second level of culture is the *transitional level*. The transitional level includes a focus on organizational rituals such as values, strategies, principles, and standards. The rituals are communicated frequently and in different formats. Many organizations try to mold their culture through their rituals but the first roadblock is that, in order for this to work, rituals have to be *shared*. For example, the CEO may have aspirational values, post them on the website, communicate them once or twice, and then call it a day. However, this is not enough. Employees need to be invested in them. The values need to be a part of their individual identity.

I worked for a company, Company X, that was comfortably situated at this transitional level. We all walked around with our values on wallet-sized cards. You couldn't even be hired into the company unless you studied and recited the values during the interview process. We knew that all employees were invested in the value rituals as we voluntarily carried these cards around. It was the strongest transitional culture I had ever experienced.

However, Company X never got below the culture surface. Although some values were understood on a *below the surface* level, there were a couple of pivotal ones that were out of alignment. For example, one of the organizational values was teamwork and collaboration—but in reality, the company was extremely individualistic and competitive. People were out for themselves, and this behavior was reinforced through the performance process. We were all force-ranked against our peers. Raises, advancement opportunities, and even access to senior leaders were all based on your ranking. We were all a number, and that number transcended everything. People would steal each other's work, take credit for what wasn't theirs, backstab one another, and even sabotage each other.

What kept Company X stuck on the transitional level is that they reaped extreme benefits for its surface and progressive transitional efforts. It was recognized around the world as an admired and great company. But when they got in the trenches, there was a different story to be told. Before they realized this, it was too late. Company X eventually flew under the radar.

The *Below the Surface* Culture Level

The deepest area of culture and the hardest to access is the *below the surface* level. This corresponds to the deepest levels of the ocean. It's uncomfortable, scary, difficult to predict, tricky to navigate—and it's very unfamiliar. I sometimes refer to the deepest levels as the muck at the bottom of the ocean.

It's the places that we don't explore because they are difficult to get to. I said it before and I will say it again:

You can't truly understand, mold, or change your culture if you are operating at a surface level.

Like the ocean, you have to go to the deepest, most uncomfortable, and murkiest areas. This might sound daunting but getting *below the surface* is only the *beginning* of the journey.

The commonality between organizations that regularly get below the culture surface is that they routinely practice *below the surface* behaviors. These organizations almost always imbue things like psychological safety, empathy, and active listening *in* their values. *Below the surface* behaviors constantly release assumptions so they are not caught in a pervasive undercurrent. I'm including a chart to help you understand the difference between transitional and *below the surface* culture levels. These are some examples that I see the most and will likely resonate with many of you.

Transitional Culture Level	*Below the Surface* Culture Level
Administering employee culture surveys	Including questions you ask in culture surveys in peer and manager 1:1s
Facilitating focus groups	Creating psychologically safe conversations about culture
Implementing a culture workshop series	Interacting with colleagues across the organization to shape, discuss, and apply values and rituals
Implementing diversity training	Practicing *below the surface* behaviors with your colleagues (psychological safety, empathetic listening, applying REAL leader concepts)

I can't stress this enough. You can't understand or mold culture if you don't get below the culture surface. If there is a discrepancy between what your organization says its culture is and what employees actually experience, it's because everything you have is aspirational. You might have enticing artifacts, shared values on paper, and maybe even a kick-ass strategy. However, if you are not accessing the level in which all of these structures manifest, none of these things are worth much. The good news is that you are two-thirds of the way there, so it's time to take that next step ahead.

Taking Action: Choosing a Track that Works for You

As we wrap up this chapter, I'm realizing that many of you may feel overwhelmed by it. Some of you may read this and think:

> "Thanks LaTonya, but this doesn't apply to me. I want to work in a *below the surface* culture but the only way to do that is to leave my company as I can't do this single-handedly."

I'm going to challenge you naysayers on this very point, but first I have a disclaimer. If you are in a severely unhealthy, toxic environment, then leaving might be your best bet. Use this book to help you identify the next *below the surface* company you want to work for.

As for the rest of you, I want to remind you we all have more power than we think we do in life. We choose where we work and how we react in those environments. The trick is accessing our power and finding ways to channel it. We first have to distinguish the levels of power to acknowledge the power we have.

If you are a professional in the workplace, there is one piece of power we all often underutilize, and that's the power to **make choices**. That's right. We choose what we want in life. Some of us may be more decisive in choosing what we want. Others of us may have more privilege so we can make our choices more swiftly than others. Some of us can afford to make riskier choices than others. Some may have the opportunity to make more choices than others. The truth of the matter though is that we all *choose*. We choose whether we speak up or cower. We choose how we react to adversity. We choose whether we want to stay at an organization or leave it. We choose if we want to attempt to change a culture in our organization. We also choose if we want to believe that we can either a) influence the space we are in or b) find the right space that fits for us.

Options are available on whichever track you choose. Whether you are focusing on getting below the culture surface in your current organization or a future one, you have a few choices in how to approach it to make it more manageable.

1) The first track you have is to focus on changing a **sub-culture** in your organization. Several culture authors actually speak of subcultures or team cultures—that one of the most powerful and accessible ways you can make change is to change your team culture. If you are a manager, you particularly have surefire ways to access *below the surface* level interactions so you can mold your culture on a micro level. Leading a team means you have the opportunity to go below the culture surface every day and insulate your environments, either permanently or

until your larger organization gets around to doing the same. Change often starts at the team level. So, if you are a manager who wants to get below the culture surface, start with your team.

2) The second track is the **individual track**. If you are an individual contributor with no direct reports, this section is for you. Maybe you never want direct reports, maybe you are just starting out in your career, or maybe you are somewhere in between. Whatever your situation, you can take the individual track and influence change accordingly. What does influencing change as an individual contributor look like? I will first tell you what it doesn't look like—taking culture change on single-handedly. You will get too emotionally involved and burnt out. Start small with these few specific actions:

- Channel your passion into asking for new culture structures instead of dwelling on old structures.
- Start a culture task force within your team. Focus on something well scoped out so you can work on creating small-scale change. If you are more aligned and committed to your team than your overall organization, you may want to start and stop your task force at the team level.
- Individually get below the culture surface through practicing P2B listening. Report your findings back to your boss.

These suggestions only work if you are passionate about your organization and are committed to making things better. Use your energy wisely. Perhaps others will do the legwork once they experience some success.

The bottom line is that you can influence more than you think as an individual.

3) The third and most obvious track is the "go big or go home" approach—changing your entire **organization**. You are committing to large-scale, multi-year efforts. Maybe you are a CEO or you lead a large organization, and thus you have this power. Four points of advice for those on this track: The first is to bring in outside help who can observe what happens below the culture surface. Second, focus on teams. Too many organizations attempt to install culture on an enterprise level all at once. While those actions are important early on, focus on how leaders can get *below the surface* within their own teams. Third, be patient. This all takes time. Fourth, remember to build flexibility into your plans. Try not to be one of those organizations that fully bakes everything up front and doesn't allow for adjustments.

My Request of You: Get Below the Culture Surface

We covered a lot in this chapter, and there is a vast amount of information to digest. So I want to end with some actionable steps you can take to get below the culture surface. With that as a summary, the next steps you want to take are to:

1) **Understand what level your organization is on:** Use the chart below for a quick three-point diagnosis of where you are. Pick the grouping that most strongly resonates with you. More tools are available at leadingbelowthesurface.com.

Surface Culture Level
- My organization is mainly focused on how we look to outside stakeholders.
- While our values are on our website, we don't reference them in day-to-day conversations.
- There is a disconnect between what my organization communicates to the outside and what employees experience on the inside.

Transitional Culture Level
- Our employees know what our values are but don't truly identify with them.
- Our surface talent processes don't align with our *below the surface* aspirations.
- Most philosophies in our organization feel aspirational and not real.

Below the Surface Culture Level
- Employees are energized by our organization's rituals.
- Managers spend most of their time in REAL interactions with their staff.
- Everything is truly "shared;" it's not just words on a piece of paper.

2) **Pick Your Track for Change:** Remember that whether you are on the individual, team, or organizational track, you can make a difference.

3) **Make a Plan:** Are you an individual contributor or manager who wants to focus on the team culture in front of you? Are you someone in a position of power or a leader who wants to change your entire organization? No matter what level you are on, make your plan for change. Start off with teams; next, move to structures; and, finally, take on systems.

Summary

Similar to the process of becoming a *below the surface leader*, if you want to get below the culture surface, you first have to understand what level you are on. Remember that the main objective is to get below the culture surface. Only there can you access what is really happening. Practicing P2B listening will quickly help you get below the culture surface. This is an often skipped step and is why many organizations quickly plateau.

The next chapter is about using *below the surface* as an effective DEIB strategy. Although it's all a part of culture, I dedicated a chapter to this topic since it's such an important issue.

10

Leading Below the Surface as an Effective DEIB Strategy

Diversity, Equity, and Inclusion (DEI)
Belonging
Inclusion, Diversity, Equity, and Access (IDEA)
Diversity & Inclusion (D&I)

That's sure a lot of words and acronyms to remember, and they are ever-evolving. Some people even switch the letters around in order of priority. There are nuances to keep track of. As I have written throughout the book, I'm going to go with DEIB to keep it simple and encompassing—Diversity, Equity, Inclusion, and Belonging. Here are my definitions of each as they pertain to *below the surface leadership* and the workplace.

> **Diversity:** Hiring and retaining different types of people. This can range from people of different races to people who think differently, and everything in between. Diversity

doesn't pertain to one race or identity; it truly is a catch-all term.

Equity: As also discussed in the REAL leadership approach, this means that people (especially othered folks) have access to what they need to be successful in an organization. In order for an organization to be equitable, people need access to people, places, resources, and spaces so they can do their jobs well and prosper.

Inclusion: If you have inclusive practices, then you enable diversity to thrive. In inclusive cultures, people are included, their presence matters, they have a voice, and space is shared.

Belonging: Belonging takes inclusion a step further. If you have belonging in the workplace, then when employees who are typically othered walk in, they immediately feel a sense of being included and being in a home-like environment. Our sense of belonging is often based on what we observe and experience within our workplaces. For example, my go-to way to understand if I belong is to look around: Does anyone look or dress like me? Do people acknowledge me? Am I seen? Am I appreciated for my strengths? All of these questions are typical to assess the level in which someone belongs at work.

2020 was a record year for DEIB. The impetus? Well, America's systemic racism repeatedly infiltrated homes all over the world. Several Black Americans were murdered at the hands of white police officers. White people watched in shock while Black folks' deaths were widely broadcasted. Due to the pandemic, we were trapped in our homes and couldn't escape. All of us had to see it. The main question swirling around in our heads: How could a defenseless Black man, George Floyd, be shamelessly murdered by a police officer in broad daylight while the entire world watched? Why didn't anyone do anything?

I will tell you something that you may have repeatedly heard last year: Black folks were not surprised in the least. This brutal murder stirred up trauma for us, and it was amplified because we were all stuck in our homes with little access to resources to help us heal.

In 2020, we all were at our wits' end. Black folks started unapologetically speaking up and telling the truth about our experiences. We wanted white people to know that this wasn't an isolated incident. Our unfiltered stories flooded the internet. For some of us, we were freely speaking out for the first time—and it was with raw emotions, at that.

Organizations were ashamed and overwhelmed with guilt. Some wanted to channel their power into change. I received phone calls from several companies that were struggling with how to respond. They had been trained to not bring "politics" into the workplace, but this didn't feel like a partisan issue to them. Their families participated in protests for the very first time in their lives. That experience forged a new perspective, one that prompted existential questions in both work and life:

- How have we not focused more on systemic racism in our organization?
- Why haven't we ever realized our privilege?
- How can we start to make real change at home and at work?

Companies realized the unbearable challenges that Black people faced and vowed to make monumental changes.

They even started embracing terms like anti-racism and intersectionality, and some even started actually caring about trans folks. What started as radical language quickly made its way to being socially accepted, everyday lexicon. But, like many existential crises, while some organizations responded from a real place, others frantically responded with *surface cultural behaviors*. They wanted to take actions that the public could see. The discomfort was too much to bear, and action was the remedy. They wanted to make quick wins and grab the low-hanging fruit. Climbing for the fruit would take too much time and distraction. They wanted the pain to stop. Some went as far as making empty promises that they could never follow through with. It was egregious.

I often reference the Kübler-Ross Change Curve in my keynotes.[36] It is a tool I use to explain the need to walk through mucky, uncomfortable experiences. The curve was originally developed to describe five key stages of grief, but it has since been adapted for organizations. According to the curve, the five steps in the change process are as follows: denial, anger, bargaining, depression, and acceptance. One can fluctuate and jump around in the curve during the grief process. For example, someone may fluctuate between anger and depression or between bargaining and denial. I also often see eager folks appearing to skip ahead, leapfrogging all the steps and heading straight towards acceptance. This is because we all want that *surface surge*, that quick boost that we get from going around something and coming up with the quickest, most performative solution. We avoid sinking into

---

[36]Elisabeth Kübler-Ross and David Kessler, *On Grief and Grieving: Finding the Meaning of Grief through the Five Stages of Loss* (New York: Scribner, 2014).

the muck (depression) even though this is where we can most easily connect *below the surface*, in our most vulnerable state.

> ## Let's Reflect
>
> Let's do some reflection. Take a few minutes to think of the last time you made a big life change prompted by grief. Write it down.

I'll go first. My big life change was losing my parents at a relatively young age, both in my 30s. Similar to many others, I went through a phase where I questioned everything. What was my real purpose in life? What really mattered? But to find answers, I had to submerge myself in the muck. The only way to the other side was to swim through it. Otherwise, that very acceptance I was seeking would only be temporary. Quickly muscling through wasn't going to work. The entire process was grimy, but I came out on the other side with a new sense of purpose. I wouldn't have discovered that purpose if I didn't endure that very abyss.

You may have had similar realizations during your reflection. I know that my clients do; they hire me when they unsuccessfully attempt to leapfrog growth stages. You can only attempt to jump so far before you hurt yourself. We saw this same avoidance of the muck play out publicly in this supposed DEIB awakening. Instead of truly reckoning with what was going on in the world, companies jumped on the performative bandwagon. Their actions appeared to be *surface*. Many companies were releasing diversity statements alongside frantically hiring Chief Diversity Officers for the first time. Remember what we said about surface behaviors?

They are superficial actions, things we do mainly because people can see we are doing them. It's like bringing the most expensive toy to show and tell.

When organizations quickly flaunt surface actions, there is always reason to be skeptical. Don't get me wrong; it was encouraging to see organizations publicly throw resources at systemic racism. But at the same time, I questioned if these actions were coming from the right place. I also questioned the timing. Why now? And if your organization couldn't support such a cause before, how can it suddenly do so now? There had to be a more real way.

The *Below the Surface* Mindset as an Effective DEIB Strategy

The amazing Angela Davis once said, "Your most important work is usually not seen."[37] This quote describes the essence of applying a *below the surface* mindset to address DEIB needs. It's a long game, and most of your work won't be "seen" at scale for quite some time. Individuals may notice, but it's going to take a while before your organization is widely recognized.

Many organizations are uncomfortable with the wait, and I get it. A surface billboard that showcases your so-called commitment to DEIB is much more seductive than a billboard insisting that your leaders stay *below the surface*. This is especially true, for example, of billboards that show executives or employees doing service in underrepresented

---

[37] Angela Davis, "A Call to Action: Then and Now" (Where Do We Go From Here: Social Justice Conference virtual keynote address, Indiana University, January 18, 2021).

communities. It's sad that DEIB can become a performance for spectators. It would be useful for us all to take a step back and yield to Davis' advice; our most important work is not seen. I would argue that the more you need it to be seen, the more you should question your intentions.

If the outside looks too good to be true, then it probably is. I learned this lesson during my late teenage years when I went with my mother to pick out my second car. I was going to be going away to college, so my mom wanted me to have a car that was a bit more reliable than my washed-out Dodge Omni. I remember looking around the lot with her and picking out a black Ford Escort. I pushed for that car as I really liked the color on the outside. There were no noticeable scratches or dents, and it felt like a huge upgrade from my tired Omni. My mom had a budget and allowed me to make the final decision (as long as I stuck to the budget), and the next day, the car was mine.

However, I soon noticed that this car was not much of an upgrade after all. It felt like it had problems right off the bat. In the first year, I probably put $2,000 into it. That's a lot for a freshman in college. The outside was immaculate, but that did not match the inside. From that point on, I knew that if the outside seemed too perfect, it would be smart to dig deeper. The outside was the surface, and getting inside was the way to access all things *below the surface.*

So what does applying *below the surface* as a DEIB strategy to get to the insides look like? Like culture, your DEIB strategy has no hope when you are on the surface. We first have to spend some real time in that muck. Yes, all of us. I've said it before and I will say it again: We can't even access *below the surface* behaviors without meandering in the muck. Diversity trainings, audits, or organizational assessments will not save you from it. You can only press the snooze button so many times.

There are four considerations we all need to take to get *below the surface* with DEIB:

1) Meander in the muck.
2) Commit to change.
3) Accept *below the surface leadership* as a legit leadership archetype.
4) Get *below the team surface.*

Meander in the Muck

Meandering in the muck is probably the most underrated and under-actioned behavior in the entire *below the surface* approach. Meandering in the muck is exactly what it sounds like. It's getting comfortable with camping out in the deepest and most uncomfortable sludge that diversity brings into the workplace. It takes a lot of vulnerability and courage to meander in the muck, and many of us, even so-called DEIB experts, avoid this experience at all costs. You can't truly create a culture of belonging if you can't meander in the muck because it's in that very muck where you can access *below the surface* spaces. No muck, no access. Many of us are quick to point our fingers at others who aren't meandering in the muck when we don't do it ourselves. Sorry, DEIB experts, but this includes all of us. I even thought that all of my othered identities exempted me from meandering in the muck—but early in my entrepreneurial journey, I learned that was not the case.

I was delivering a private keynote called "How to Be an Amazing Ally." It was Pride Month, so I focused on allyship for LGBTQ+ folks. After the session, I got the usual glowing compliments. For many people, this was the first time they had ever fully understood the word "allyship," so many of the comments were wrapped in inspiration. But there was one comment that I will always remember. It was career changing. I had a person approach me in obvious distress about something that I said. Their voice cracked when they spoke. And they delivered me a shit sandwich on the spot: "Your presentation was great but—I'm not sure you realized this—I heard you say 'transgenders.' The correct word is transgender. But again, the presentation was great."

I couldn't hear anything but "transgenders." My ability to P2P listen evaporated on the spot. It was really hard to hear that, and my somatic response in my body was defensiveness. No way did I say "transgenders." I had done this presentation several times before today. They must have heard me wrong. But at that moment, I realized that the situation was mucky. I could not see in front or in back of me. I knew that part of my growth was surrendering to the muck. I was in the pit, and it was at that moment that I could access *below the surface* spaces. So, instead of responding with defensiveness, I said, "Thank you for providing me with that honest perspective. I didn't even realize it and I will get better."

I refrained from defensiveness or 'splaining. I knew that while the muck was unbelievably excruciating, it was where I needed to be. This is what meandering in the muck looks like: getting there and staying there—not responding with surface defenses. You can't successfully move to solutioning without camping out in the muck, so get your best gear ready. I want to reiterate that the muck is the most needed and hardest place to be in. If you want to create real cultures of belonging, try meandering in the muck on a regular basis.

Commit to Change

The second consideration to get *below the surface* with DEIB is to commit to real change. Two key actions are at play here. The first is to commit. The second part is committing to change. Let's explore the first one, commitment. Before I go into what that looks like, I want you all to do a quick reflection.

Let's Reflect

When was the last time you committed to something you succeeded at?

What did you experience when you made that commitment:

1) In your mind?
2) In your body?

This is an important exercise, so take a few minutes to truly reflect here. I will share my example: writing this very book. My commitment to writing it went beyond saying it out loud. It also went beyond putting it on my to-do list. I had to *hold space* for it. I started with one-hour writing sessions and then worked up from there. But it was bigger than making the time for it: I had to hold space for it in my mind, body, and spirit. That meant clearing other non-value-added things from my life. When I talked about the book after I fully committed, it felt like an integral part of my life, not simply a side project. When I committed to it, I felt a sense of embodiment. The book became a part of me. I lived and breathed it.

One last point I will make on this: Simply making the commitment was a step within itself. Nobody was telling me what to do. I had to commit, and it was a process.

Now back to the reflection. What was your commitment? How did you feel in your mind and body when you made that commitment? What was your process?

The reason why it's important to make this connection is because the way that you committed to *yourself* is the same way you will need to commit to change in *your organization*. We have to ask our leaders to commit, and this goes beyond rattling off the current DEIB strategy. They are committing to change, change that they are experiencing in their own mind, body, and spirit. That's all. So it's important to not clutter our heads with memorizing vision and strategy statements in this early stage. Literally all you need to do is commit.

Now that we have experienced what it's like to make a commitment, the second step is to commit to a certain type of change. Ask yourself what change you want to make. It's not necessary to make a checklist here. A few questions you might want to consider:

- What will your organization look like if the change is successful?
- How do you know when your organization is steering off the tracks?
- How can you incorporate this change into your daily practices?

Thoroughly consider what the change looks and feels like. Focus on what it looks like and *how* you will experience it, not *what* it is. Again, this is the time to avoid checklists. You have to embody the change. That's what real commitment involves.

Accept *Below the Surface Leadership* as a Legit Leadership Archetype

The third consideration to make is to accept *below the surface leadership* as a legitimate leadership archetype. Early in my career, I participated in a few different leadership accelerators. In one of these so-called profound sessions, the topic was "leadership archetypes." In this course, we were presented with a survey that would assess what kind of leader we were. We would then be mapped to one of seven leadership archetypes, such as the strategist, the innovator, the fixer, the builder—the list went on. I was a builder. I liked to build new things. Yes, this was correct. That's exactly what I was. I always had an entrepreneurial orientation, so it was good that this was finally confirmed and that my organization would see me this way as well. Everything should be fine now.

Right?

Wrong. Something continued to bother me about this the entire process. First off, I felt like boxing me into one of these types was forceful and unorthodox. I was more complex. How could I be in one box? Secondly, there wasn't a single archetype that discussed our deepest leadership intentions. That didn't matter in this approach. For example, I could build lots of stuff but I could have odious intentions. So what if you were strategic? You could be a strategic narcissist.

I participated in many more of these leadership experiences throughout the years and they were all the same. Name your work style assessment, and I have participated. Every single one was also missing a characterization of the leader who achieves results based on how we treat people or the extent to which we get *below the surface*. None of them prioritized *how* we treat people. Leadership was built on prototypes, and nothing that even resembled REAL leadership behaviors were on the list.

This experience was among the first in which I realized that, as discussed in Chapter 2, the widely accepted leadership standard was shallow and surface. We fundamentally had to revisit how we defined and measured leadership. While inclusion is important, it's usually presented as something separate from fundamental leadership archetypes and historically has not been regarded as a fundamental archetype like "innovation" or "strategy." It's nice to have but that's about all. The way it has been treated goes like this: *Well, now that we've grown enough, maybe we should focus on diversity.* It's the side, not the main dish, and by then it's too late. While inclusive leadership is better than nothing, many definitions of it don't explicitly include *below the surface* behaviors, such as awareness and equity. *Below the surface leadership* is an archetype, so if you want to move forward in your DEIB efforts, accept it and build it into all of your manager and leader development.

Getting *Below the Team Surface*

We have already spent a great deal of time discussing individual tactics to get *below the surface* in Chapter 4, so let's shift to teams. Let's first explore in more detail why focusing on teams is beneficial.

According to *HBR*, the amount of time employees spend engaged in collaborative work increased roughly 50% over the last two decades.[38] Employees are on twice as many teams

---

[38]Rob Cross, Reb Rebele, and Adam Grant, "Collaborative Overload," *Harvard Business Review*, January–February 2016, https://hbr.org/2016/01/collaborative-overload.

as they were five years ago.[39] Since teams are where we spend most of our time, they offer a valuable opportunity to apply *below the surface* concepts.

Teams represent a microcosm of organizational DEIB efforts, so if you want to assess how your organization is doing, evaluate how your teams are doing. Microcultures are bred in teams. An organization can be made up of several microcultures. Employees even interchange their descriptions of their organizations' microcultures and macrocultures. For example, it's common for employees at large companies to have markedly different experiences within their team as opposed to the larger organization.

Now, back to getting below the team surface. How do we make this happen in practice? To answer this question, I want to share some observations from my experience coaching teams. Some of the biggest reasons why I see teams fail at getting *below the surface* are a lack of purpose, lack of clear roles, strained relationships, and lack of process. What's the recourse? Many folks would tell you to organize a team retreat or to even bring in a consultant to run some assessments on the team. I'm not saying that you shouldn't do these things, but we often skip getting *below the surface* before we dive into solutions.

Getting below the team surface involves taking a step back, observing team interactions, practicing P2P listening, practicing P2B listening, and being willing to sink into the muck at any given time. Instead of reaching for the stars in terms of your team DEIB goals, try starting off observing and

---

[39] "A Foundation for Modern Collaboration: Microsoft 365 Bolsters Teamwork," Microsoft Corporation, May 16, 2018, https://www.microsoft.com/en-us/itshowcase/a-foundation-for-modern-collaboration-microsoft-365-bolsters-teamwork.

evaluating the extent to which REAL behaviors are displayed on your team. Is the team a surface unit? Use Chapter 4 as a resource to understand the extent to which your team is getting *below the surface*.

Summary: My Request of You

Now that you have read this chapter, I want to request that you take out a sheet of paper. Make four columns: activity, *below the surface*, transitional, and surface. In the activity column, list everything that you (or your organization) have done in the past to foster DEIB in your organization. Everything you know of. Once your activity list is done, ask yourself if the activity was *below the surface, transitional, or surface level.* Put a check in the corresponding column. Sit with your list to allow time to meander in the muck.

Now, I want you to pick two of the approaches that I introduced in this chapter to focus on going forward. As a reminder, the four main approaches introduced in this chapter are as follows:

1) Meander in the muck.
2) Commit to change.
3) Accept *below the surface leadership* as a legit leadership archetype.
4) Get *below the team surface.*

CHAPTER 11

We Can All Do This— Managing Your *Below the Surface* Journey Ahead

So, folks, this brings us to our final chapter. Let's focus on an important topic: managing your unique *below the surface* journey going forward. As we discussed throughout this book, real connection is at the root of *leading below the surface*. This type of genuine connection can be accessed within any type of organization or team to create a complete cultural shift. *Leading below the surface* provides a structured system that anyone can practice and rely on for years to come. Superficiality will be long gone once you are submerged *below the surface*. We are all capable of it.

Now for a disclaimer. I'm not going to claim that embodying *below the surface* approaches will single-handedly cure systemic oppressions in the workplace. Curing systemic oppressions will require coordinated multidisciplinary approaches that go well beyond your organizations.

I was once in a team coaching session when one of the leaders said something that stuck with me, "While we can't cure systemic racism in this room, there are a lot of things we can cure in our company." That resonated with his team. With everyone. He wanted his team to first get *below the surface* and identify what they could change. He wanted to avoid grandiose promises. He wanted to be realistic and focus on what was in front of him and his executive team.

We can all change what's in front of us, but we first have to activate the power that we do have to shift inequities within our own organizations. Let's first address what's within our purview before we carry the weight of the world on our shoulders. We all want the world to get better, but sometimes we abandon the small day-to-day wins to go after the larger billboard items. Shifts happen one team at a time.

I have shared some vulnerable stories of my experiences, but this book isn't about me. It's about making the world a better place. It's about making organizations more equitable. It's about breaking structures and building new ones. I have provided you with the knowledge to do exactly that. Taking action is up to you. When you feel like you are floundering in your *below the surface* journey, practice one of these lifelines:

- Spot and speak out against the terrible three to create an increased sense of belonging in your organizations.
- Embody REAL leader behaviors to get you back on track, especially when you are having trouble building relationships with people who are different from you.
- Acknowledge that we will always be up against a surface world.
- Accept empathy and psychological safety as the engines of *below the surface* cultures.
- Recognize that you have to get *below the surface* if you want to do real DEIB work and, eventually, change your culture.

This book is not a blueprint on how to be a *below the surface leader*. Take what you want from these chapters, apply what works, and develop your own *below the surface leadership* style. I made a conscious choice not to make this book too calculated or complicated because everyone is different and I sincerely want to honor that. However, I think we would all agree that execution is the hardest part.

Things will get hard. You will want to throw it all out. You will want to go back to old habits. You will have slips. We all do! However, it's important to remember that we are all in this together. Share your slips with another aspiring *below the surface leader*. Also share your successes. Build an indestructible community to keep you on par.

I will leave you with these real and encouraging words:

We can *all* do this.
This is *our* time to influence *our* organizations.
Below the surface leadership is leadership.

My business coach always used to say, "You make my day when you share your successes." At first, I thought she was merely being polite, but then, throughout my work, I experienced the same phenomenon. It would make my day when my clients shared successes with me. I'm looking forward to all of you making my day. Don't hesitate to drop me a note if you want to share successes or challenges. I will make every effort possible to read all of them.

One final note: go back and review chapters, as needed. This book was written so each could stand alone based on your needs. If you need REAL leader inspiration, go back to Chapter 4. If you are feeling alone in a surface world, go back to Chapter 5. If you are trying to make real culture and DEIB change in your organization, study Chapters 7–10. There's something here for everyone.

I look forward to being inspired by all of you.

**P.S More tools and resources are available at latonyawilkins.com or leadingbelowthesurface.com

Conclusion

Thank you for reading *Leading Below the Surface*. Now that you have gotten to this point, please consider leaving me a review on Amazon or Goodreads so others can easily find *Leading Below the Surface*. This book is only the start of your *below the surface* transformation. Let's continue to partner on your journey. Here's how we can stay in touch.

Web: latonyawilkins.com or leadingbelowthesurface.com
Instagram: @latonyacoaching
LinkedIn: linkedin.com/in/latonyawilkins
Twitter: @latonyawilkins

On my website, you'll find free tools and resources for you and your organization, an outline of my speaking topics, and more information on scheduling time to speak with me for coaching and consultation. I look forward to connecting with you.

Acknowledgments

I acknowledge my family, friends, and community who were there with me at different points throughout this process. Special thanks to my longtime friend, Eric, who introduced me to a book attorney so I could navigate the publishing industry. I also want to acknowledge my friends and colleagues who preceded me in writing something significant—providing me with the necessary reassurance so I believed I could complete such a big project. Thank you for providing me the support, especially in the times when I was falling off a ledge. There are way too many of you to name here.

I want to thank everyone who pitched into the editing process, including longtime friends and clients.

I appreciate all of the folks who have mentored me throughout my life, including Sherry, my longtime friend and coach. I am thankful for all of my early college instructors who believed in my writing. I also want to thank Lisa for helping me keep my mental health intact.

Thank you to my partner, Tiffeny, who provided me with emotional support throughout the process. I appreciate your reassurance in the most difficult of times.

Other special thanks to:

Amy Edmondson for writing my foreword.
Suzi Steffen for all of your expertise.
My staff and contractors at the Change Coaches.
All of my clients.
My gym, Urban Athlete, for keeping the community going in 2020. That was my only escape.
To all of my friends who talked me off a ledge during this process—there are too many to name here.
All my coach writing groups (especially my BIPOC folks).
To all of my friends and supporters who made valuable connections for me throughout this process especially Debra, Jane, Denise, Jana, and Blythe.
Everyone who supported my book launch.
To everyone who has purchased this book or supported me in other ways.
My colleagues at the Gies College of Business who have supported my journey.
My higher power, who guided me spiritually from afar.

And, finally, to Publish Your Purpose—thanks for guiding me through the process and making it possible for me to write this book on my terms.

About the Author

Founder of The Change Coaches, LaTonya Wilkins partners with executives, upwardly mobile professionals, and teams to build cultures of belonging through highly customized coaching and consulting services. She is a sought-after keynote speaker and has inspired audiences all over the world. She built her career working in HR,  talent management, and learning and development at Fortune 500 companies before teaching and taking on progressive leadership roles at the University of Illinois' Gies College of Business. LaTonya is currently the President of the True Star Youth Foundation board. She gained industry recognition when she was featured on the peer-nominated list of most inclusive HR influencers in 2019.

LaTonya developed her signature concept of Below the Surface Leadership based on her own experience climbing the corporate ladder and researching across disciplines while constantly being the "only one" on her teams. This revolutionary approach to leadership is about creating psychologically safe relationships across differences; empowering underrepresented employees to feel valued, heard, and engaged; and creating cultures of belonging in the workplace.

LaTonya's clients often describe her as approachable, non-judgmental, inspiring, creative, unique, and insightful. You may experience her the same way as you read through *Leading Below the Surface*.

Bibliography

A Workplace Divided: Understanding the Climate for LGBTQ Workers Nationwide. Human Rights Campaign, 2018. https://www.hrc.org/resources/aworkplace-divided-understanding-the-climate-for-lgbtqworkers-nationwide.

Bartol, Kathryn M., Charles L. Evans, and Melvin T. Stith. "Black versus White Leaders: A Comparative Review of the Literature." *The Academy of Management Review* 3, no. 2 (April 1978): 293–304.

Bullard, Eric A. "Queer Leadership: A Phemonological Study of the Experiences of Out and Gay Lesbian Higher Education Presidents." PhD dissertation, Colorado State University, 2013.

CareerBuilder. "More Than One-Quarter of Managers Said They Weren't Ready to Lead When They Began Managing Others, Finds New CareerBuilder Survey." PR Newswire, March 28, 2011. http://press.careerbuilder.com/2011-03-28-More-Than-OneQuarter-of-Managers-Said-They-Werent-Ready-toLead-When-They-Began.

Castilla, Emilio J. "Gender, Race, and Meritocracy in Organizational Careers." *American Journal of*

Sociology 113, no. 6 (May 2008): 1479–526. https://doi.
org/10.1086/588738.

Cooper, Marianne. "The False Promise of Meritocracy."
The Atlantic, December 1, 2015. https://www.
theatlantic.com/business/archive/2015/12/
meritocracy/418074/.

Cross, Rob, Reb Rebele, and Adam Grant. "Collaborative
Overload." *Harvard Business Review*, January–
February 2019. https://hbr.org/2016/01/
collaborative-overload.

Davis, Angela. "A Call to Action: Then and Now." Where
Do We Go From Here: Social Justice Conference virtual
keynote address, Indiana University, January 18, 2021.

Devine, Patricia, Patrick S. Forscher, Anthony J. Austin, and
William T. L. Cox. "Long-Term Reduction in Implicit
Race Bias: A Prejudice Habit-Breaking Intervention."
Journal of Experimental Social Psychology 46, no. 6
(November 2012): 1267–78. https://doi.org/10.1016/j.
jesp.2012.06.003.

Edmondson, Amy C. *The Fearless Organization: Creating
Psychological Safety in the Workplace for Learning,
Innovation, and Growth.* Hoboken, N.J.: John Wiley &
Sons, 2018. Kindle.

"Glassdoor Survey Finds Three in Five U.S. Employees
Have Experienced or Witnessed Discrimination Based
on Age, Race, Gender or LGBTQ at Work." Glassdoor,
October 23, 2019. https://about-content.glassdoor.com/
en-us/diversity-inclusion-2019/.

Gosfeld-Nir, Abraham, Boaz Ronen, and Nir Kozlovsky.
"The Pareto Managerial Principle: When Does It
Apply?" *International Journal of Production Research*
45, no. 10 (May 2007): 2317–25.

Groysberg, Boris, Jeremiah Lee, Jessie Price, and J. Yo-Jud Cheng. "The Leader's Guide to Corporate Culture." *Harvard Business Review*, January–February 2018. https://hbr.org/2018/01/the-leaders-guide-to-corporate-culture.

Kirkland, Rik, and Iris Bohnet. "Focusing on What Works for Workplace Diversity." McKinsey & Company, April 7, 2017. https://www.mckinsey.com/featured-insights/gender-equality/focusing-on-what-works-for-workplace-diversity.

Kübler-Ross, Elisabeth, and David Kessler. *On Grief and Grieving: Finding the Meaning of Grief Through the Five Stages of Loss*. London: Simon & Schuster, 2014.

Maslow, Abraham. "A Theory of Human Motivation." *Psychology Review* 50, no. 4 (1943): 370–96.

Microsoft Corporation. "A Foundation for Modern Collaboration: Microsoft 365 Bolsters Teamwork." May 16, 2018. https://www.microsoft.com/en-us/itshowcase/a-foundation-for-moderncollaboration-microsoft-365-bolsters-teamwork.

Morad, Natali. "Part 1: How to Be an Adult—Kegan's Theory of Adult Development." Medium, September 28, 2017. https://medium.com/@NataliMorad/how-tobe-an-adult-kegans-theory-of-adult-developmentd63f4311b553.

Nalty, Kathleen. "Strategies for Confronting Unconscious Bias." *Federal Lawyer* 64, no. 1 (January/February 2017): 26–34.

O'Reilly, Charles. "Corporations, Culture and Commitment: Motivation and Social Control in Organizations." *California Management Review* 31, no. 4 (July 1989): 9–25.

Phillips, Katherine W., Tracy L. Dumas, and Nancy P. Rothbard. "Diversity and Authenticity." *Harvard Business Review*, March–April 2018. https://hbr.org/2018/03/diversity-and-authenticity.

Riordan, Christine. "Three Ways Leaders Can Listen with More Empathy." *Harvard Business Review*, January 16, 2014. https://hbr.org/2014/01/three-ways-leaders-can-listen-with-more-empathy.

Roberts, Morgan, Anthony J. Mayo, Robin J. Ely, and David A. Thomas. "Beating the Odds." *Harvard Business Review*, March–April 2018. https://hbr.org/2018/03/beating-the-odds.

Rosette, Ashleigh S., Geoffrey J. Leonardelli, and Katherine W. Phillips. "The White Standard: Racial Bias in Leader Categorization." *Journal of Applied Psychology* 93, no 4 (July 2008): 758–77. https://doi.org/10.1037/0021-9010.93.4.758.

Schein, Edgar H. "Coming to a New Awareness of Organizational Culture." *MIT Sloan Management Review*, Winter 1984, https://sloanreview.mit.edu/article/coming-to-a-new-awareness-of-organizational-culture/.

Scott, Allison, Freada Kapor Klein, and Uriridiakoghene Onovakpuri. *Tech Leavers Study*. Kapor Center for Social Impact, 2017. https://www.kaporcenter.org/wp-content/uploads/2017/08/TechLeavers2017.pdf.

Sinar, Evan, Rich Wellins, Matthew Paese, Audrey Smith, and Bruce Watt. *High Resolution Leadership: A Synthesis of 15,000 Assessments into How Leaders Shape the Business Landscape*. Development Dimensions International, 2016. https://media.ddiworld.com/research/high-resolution-leadership-2015-2016_tr_ddi.pdf.

So, Richard Jean, and Gus Wezerek. "Just How White Is the Book Industry?" *The New York Times*, December 11, 2020. https://www.nytimes.com/interactive/2020/12/11/opinion/culture/diversity-publishing-industry.html.

State of the American Workplace 2017. Gallup, 2017. https://www.gallup.com/workplace/238085/stateamerican-workplace-report-2017.aspx.

"*The New York Times* Business Books Best Sellers List." *The New York Times*, November 15, 2020. https://www.nytimes.com/books/best-sellers/2020/11/15/business-books/.

"Time's Most Influential Business Management Books." *Time*, August 9, 2011. http://content.time.com/time/specials/packages/completelist/0,29569,2086680,00.html.

Travis, Dnika J., and Jennifer Thorpe-Moscon. "Day-to-Day Experiences of Emotional Tax Among Women and Men of Color in the Workplace." *Catalyst*, February 15, 2018. https://www.catalyst.org/research/day-to-dayexperiences-of-emotional-tax-among-women-and-menof-color-in-the-workplace/.

Wang, Yanfei, Jieqiong Liu, and Yu Zhu. "Humble Leadership, Psychological Safety, Knowledge Sharing, and Follower Creativity: A Cross-Level Investigation." *Frontiers in Psychology* 9 (September 2018): 1727. https://doi.org/10.3389/fpsyg.2018.01727.

Weir, Kristen. "The Pain of Social Rejection." *Monitor on Psychology* 43, no. 4 (2012): 50. http://www.apa.org/monitor/2012/04/rejection.

Wu, Jade. "The Power of Oxytocin." *Psychology Today*, February 11, 2020. https://www.psychologytoday.com/us/blog/the-savvy-psychologist/202002/the-power-oxytocin.

CPSIA information can be obtained
at www.ICGtesting.com
Printed in the USA
LVHW082351250422
717159LV00004B/237